NANIN

NANIN

Tony Thornton

The Book Guild Ltd
Sussex, England

First published in Great Britain in 2001 by
The Book Guild Ltd
25 High Street
Lewes, East Sussex
BN7 2LU

Typesetting in Times by
IML Typographers, Birkenhead, Merseyside

Printed in Great Britain by
Bookcraft (Bath) Ltd, Avon

A catalogue record for this book is available from
The British Library.

ISBN 1 85776 523 0

CONTENTS

ACKNOWLEDGEMENTS

This book is dedicated to the people in my life who have kept my alive, and helped me well again.

My thanks to the doctors and nursing staff at Walsgrave Caludon Psychiatric Unit, particularly the nursing staff on Beechwood Ward, and Gulson Hospital Psychology Unit. Particular thanks to psychologists John Davies and Vathany Reginald, without whom my recovery would not have happened. Thanks to Survivors Sheffield, and to the Samaritans, many dark nights have passed successfully with help from them. Biggest thanks though to Jack and Jane, my friends. You had faith in me, and I am alive today because of your efforts. In writing this book, I think of all the other men out there who have suffered the same thing.

To them I say, 'Have faith; in yourself.'

It's also for the people in my life whom I care for.

To my sons, all my love, always.

To Lisa, I wish you only happiness.

To all the rest of my extended family, I hope you now understand.

To Aly, my heart, mind, body and soul belong to you . . .

I have finally found peace.

THE JOINING

You drift, everything is soft, warm, safe. There are no real feelings at first, a half-sleep state is your world, it fills you with safety, softness and comfort that makes up you. The other is there, and you know without knowing that you share not only your space but also your feelings, what happens to you, happens to the other and you are not alone, for the other is there . . . and you are as one.

Time passes, you grow, feelings grow, you become slowly, oh so slowly aware, what was softness becomes form, you still drift but now you begin to feel also your world and that of the other is liquid, liquid warmth, and also not only are you and the other here, you feel you are joined to the outside, not known just felt, when you feel uncomfortable, empty, you are filled from the joining, when you are full, the same takes away that feeling. You do not know just what it is, but it is your strength, your protection, it is a link to . . .? Life. Also, another feeling is there – warmth? happiness? love? Yes, love, love comes from the joining. All the things you are, your whole being and that of the other, are also of the joining. You are one but you are also separate. No words, no knowledge, just awareness.

Movement . . . wriggling, growth and filling your space, you and the other grow, the times of half-sleep are less, the times of feeling are more, you explore your world, each day brings a new feeling, a new thought, from nothing you are, with the other, becoming . . . something . . .

Bathing in comfort, becomes floating, your liquid home has walls, and as you grow you feel those walls, feel the other against you moving also in this world, growing alongside of you, part of you but separate, together but different.

1

One day, you wake from rest, after being filled from the joining, and a new feeling is there, you know the other's thoughts. There has been a massive change, not sudden but spontaneous, a natural progression has taken place, the other is there in your head and you in theirs, something has opened to make a contact, no words, no movement, just a knowing of the other's thoughts, and a bond is born so strong you know it is there forever. This world of yours, for you do not know it is your world but know a sense of being, is shared. From nothing you are, with the other and from the joining, becoming something.

Time passes.

The space you have shrinks, or maybe you are growing. The other is pressed against you now all the time and you feel the walls of your world around you constantly. There seems to be more of you (and the other), 'bits' stick out, uncomfortable in their extensions, seeming sometimes to poke out and prod the walls of your world, the other, and from there to, bits sticking out, prodding you too, life however, is still good, still warm and still safe ... mostly, for just lately as you and the other have developed, new and strange feelings have been coming to you.

The feeling of ... 'being' ... the sense of separation from the joining, of being a separate thing, also to the other, needing your own space of being a separate entity, sharing but separate, both joined to ... life? Both sharing hunger, feeding, warmth and emptying from the joining, and also feeling each other's thoughts, moods really, knowing the other's needs as you know your own, but that bond is still strong and you know instinctively the other, know them as you know yourself, and they too, know you. The link is set. The feelings and thoughts of them are there, mingled with your own. Isolation is not in your existence, not known to you – togetherness is. Right from before thoughts became firm, they are there with you. You are together.

The joining also has changed; once it just sent filling to make you not hungry and took away fullness afterwards, leaving you with satisfied sleep, contentedness. Now it sends small messages, normally it is just safeness and warmth, but now as you develop and grow you feel other things like brief times of euphoria, a feeling of being so high you could shake off this world of yours and

2

float upwards forever. Strangely though, when this feeling comes your world seems to get smaller, there seems a great pushing in of the walls about you, a heavy weight on top of you squashing your world with the other, and the joining seems to also tell you of discomfort? Of scrunching up? Feelings flow into you and the other at great speed at this time, blood beats faster through you both from the joining, pulsing waves of energy into you, stimulating parts of you both to wake up, learn, feel life within you both. An urgency takes the joining, discomfort, stimulation, 'going' somewhere at a great pace, a race, yes, a race you are feeling from the joining, but not quite part of sharing in but separate from, you squirm and move, wanting you don't know what. But knowing it is coming, feeling it second-hand from the joining, diluted, but so powerful. It almost hurts in its urgency, squashed as you are at these times, but all that doesn't matter for the euphoria that follows is worth it, worth the closeness of your world because after, when that burst like starlight explodes from the joining, coming down and hitting you like electricity, filling you and the other with an overwhelming sense of well-being and fulfilment, you drift into a sleep of euphoric splendour and feel safe and warm and ... love.

There are other times also of discomfort, not only small discomfort like when the other or you move slightly and seem to lodge in a corner and push against each other or the outside, sometimes the joining seems to feel or portray a message of discomfort and your world moves about until comfort returns, but also a larger feeling sometimes, a feeling that flows through the joining and instead of filling you to quench the emptiness it gives not food but feelings and you and the other KNOW that all is not right, that out there past the ends of your known worlds, a different thing is there. Fear? Anxiety? Yes, yes, you do not know the words but the feelings speak for themselves, a message of 'hide, run, protect', and you and the other twist and turn squirming in your fear, and sometimes a sharp pulse of feeling from the joining, terror followed by a pain, physical pain, to your world, to the joining, and you and the other writhe about not understanding as inside your world everything is warm and liquid and safe, but the joining gives a different message and gives pain from the walls of your world, but perhaps not ... perhaps the joining also feels pain from outside their walls? It is all very confusing, and you and the other struggle to comprehend, to try and settle back into safeness. But you cannot, as the messages from outside are so strong, so you feel uncomfortable and vulnerable, until exhaustion takes you and the opposite from euphoria fills your thoughts. When this happens you drift into a sleep full of concern and terror.

When you wake from these times immediately you feel about you, feel the joining, question it. Safe? Warm? And you feel back sadness, sorrow and love.

Time passes, you grow, the other grows, bonding takes place. You and the other are separate but one, you explore everything together – your world, your growth, the joining. As the bits of you grow, stick out, they bring touch and you and the other 'feel' each other, not only are they there alongside your very being, they are physically beside you also, and in this liquid warmth that is your world you feel the softness of their skin, the curve and form of their body, fingers? Yes, they are fingers these sticky-out bits, you don't actually know the words but you KNOW they are, they feel the other, the other also feels you, knows not only with their mind then but with their body also that you are together, this filters into each other's feelings and an overwhelming unshakeable knowledge grows within you.

You will never be alone; you will ALWAYS have the other.

One day your life, for that is what it now is, changes forever. Inside your world it is now very tight indeed, you and the other are curled into a ball wrapped around the confines of this space, wrapped around each other most times as there is so little space left now in your joint world. Each other's joining intertwined about the other's. The feeling of warmth not only comes from your world's liquid or the softness of the walls but also from the heat of the other, pressed now tightly against you. There seems to be a growing feeling of wanting escape, of wanting, however strange it may be, to end being in this space and to move on to another place, another larger place, another ... the outside ... yes the outside. Of wanting to go to the outside, to stretch and, and ... you don't know. You just have the feeling of wanting to go 'somewhere'. The feelings from the joining have also been strange of late, almost a feeling of eviction, but mixed with fear, of? Of wanting to release you but wanting to keep you safe also, and somehow, the outside world would not be safe. Strange feelings altogether, not 'normal' feelings, you just know that, you and the other have shared many moments together, thinking over and, yes, you are both able to think now, thinking over these feelings, but it is okay because no matter what, you have each other, even when you are outside you will still have that bond, you both know that.

A pulse comes down from the joining, urgent ... urgent ... you and the other are immediately alert, searching ... you have felt this feeling before, usually along with physical discomfort, danger. You both feel fear ... this is not a new feeling but never have you felt it so strong, you know with certainty what is to come, you and the other roll into a ball around each other, hugging, holding, wanting this feeling to pass, knowing the fear and unsafeness you must feel first before it will go, the joining twists and turns, the other too, you feel the same things, another pulse, panic ... bump, bump, bump.... The fear runs around you, pulse after pulse hits you both. No, no, no.... A massive pulse comes down from the joining, this is bad, this is very very bad. The pulse hits you both.

RUN ... HIDE ... FLEE FOR YOUR LIVES ... RUN, RUN, RUN, RUN, RUNNNNN, BANG...

The wall of your world collapses, blind panic ... you feel the other's mind, pain, pain, pain. ... The wall of your world has collapsed on them, there is a hardness instantly pressing them into their space, they are crushed, their joining has been squashed, they have been squashed, panic, panic. ... What can you do? How can you escape? You feel the other's mind, it is crying out to you; screaming to you help, help – and you can do nothing. Shock takes you, here beside you part of you; the other half of your very existence is hurting, screaming out into your mind messages of fear, of not understanding, of blind panic mixed with unbearable pain. The pain travels up the other's joining to the outside, massive hurt, help ... twist ... turn ... escape ... save me ... make me safe please ... please ... save me ... I feel it all in my head, in my thoughts; I am full of the other's pain and my own confusion and panic. A throb of strength races down from the joining, hang on, hang on, instinct, mother's instinctive strength ... I won't let this

5

happen to my ... my ... my babies. Yes we are here, babies, inside her, the other is crying out in pain. I am immobilised with fear and panic, what is happening? What can I do? My other is hurting and I can do nothing but look on with my mind at the fury and hurt that surrounds us. I feel a struggle from the outside, I feel my twin ... my twin ... I feel her thoughts because everything is crystal clear; now I know everything, we have been hit, this hurt is not from the joining but from outside our world, outside even the joining, my twin is hurt and I am okay, but that is not okay, I want to hurt too, I want to take some of this damage on to me. To take it away from her so it will not be so bad for her. My heart races, what can I do? What can I do?

I turn to my twin ... help, help, help ... races from my head to hers. I am here, I will save you. But when I feel her, I know I can't ... she is hurt bad, very bad and as I watch her feelings become one with her in her pain I feel her dying, I know she is going to go, to leave me. That unshakeable, unstoppable bond that joins us is about to be broken forever. I try to take some of her hurt from her, I move closer in the confines of our world and touch, I wrap my arms around her small body, feeling her draw back in pain as I do but thanking me with her thoughts for trying, the pain in her body wracking her, I move as close as I can to her, touching her gently to let her feel me against her as she fades, I feel her going ... her joining is crushed ... she is dying from suffocation, a slow choking fading that fills her thoughts with terror, she struggles to keep alive, I feel the thunderous roar of her blood as it struggles to keep going around her body, feel through her the horrible inevitability of what is going to happen, nothing can stop it. She looks to me in her thoughts one last time and I feel a weak pulse of warmth, of love from her, please, please don't leave me ... please don't go ... PLEASE ... she looks into me, joins for the last time with me and I feel her saying, feeling 'It's okay, I know you can't help but don't let this happen to you. Hide, hide, hide away until it's safe' ... and a final burst of thought from her ... LOVE ... and she was gone. Gone forever. An emptiness took me then like a giant black pit, bottomless, fathomless: where there had been half of me there was nothing, what had been by my side forever in my existence was no more. All I could feel with my body was a lump of dead flesh against me, not the warm living thing that had shared my world, but a cold unmoving corpse, my brain searched for its companion and found emptiness, a void where there had been life. Terror took me then ... great pain ... pulses from the outside ... what's happening? Pain and hurt and confusion and ... with me a feeling of drifting, of it being too much, of her last thoughts to me. Hide ... hide ... blackness came thankfully. I left a bit of me on guard to keep me living – and the rest of me? I hid.

THE 'PLAN'

He walked nervously up and down the corridor. 'It is going to be all right. I know it is going to be all right', he thought. Hospitals had always frightened him, he had watched his dad die slowly in a hospital just like this one, watched each day as he had withered and shrunk in front of him, he had loved his dad, not like the bastard who had taken his place in his mum's affections, no ... not like him at all. If it had been HIM lying in that hospital bed, well, that would have been COMPLETELY different. His life would have been a hell of a lot easier anyway, he wouldn't have ended up the family outcast as he was now, scorned by all of his family, alone in the world with no one to turn to in times like this.

He hated hospitals, and this one was no exception, cold white walls, hollow corridors that smelt of antiseptic and illness, he could almost imagine catching something just by breathing the air into his lungs. His dad had caught consumption, he wasn't too sure what that was but he knew they had to wear a mask when visiting him, which made things worse, it somehow removed even further the person he looked up to and worshipped ... his dad. He would cheerfully have died in his place, wished he had sometimes at the hand of his 'new' dad. New ... huh. He was not his dad, he may have married his mum, the slut, but he wasn't his dad.

How she could have married so soon after his dad's death shocked and worried him. His parents seemed to have a good relationship. Dad ruled with an iron fist, mum knew just where she stood, did the cooking and cleaning and that, and everyone was happy, weren't they? Meals were on the table at regular times, clothes were washed and pressed meticulously, the house was spotless – dad had made sure of that, he had barked and shouted enough when it wasn't, he remembered. His mum was how mums should be, soft, gentle, there for you, but behind the scenes when not wanted. Yes, it had been a good life for everyone up till then. This new one . . . huh. Mum had gone to the dogs big time, joining 'evening classes', evening classes for God's sake. What the hell could they teach her she didn't already know about housework? What else DID she need to know? Nothing as far as he was concerned, as far as his dad was concerned too and his dad was ALWAYS right in his eyes. He and his mum had never seen eye to eye after that, it seemed to be one big round of him trying to keep up the standards his dad had instigated, and one big fight from her and this . . . prick she had married, not to. Every single time he had come home the place would be a mess, he had to wait for two or three days sometimes for his clothes to be washed and worse still had even had to IRON stuff himself sometimes. The new bloke seemed to be happy with this, he had heard him once telling his mum not to run around after the kid, that he was old enough to get his own stuff. What the hell were mothers for then if not to look after their children?

He hated the new bloke, hated him with a vengeance. He had taken his dad's place, was sleeping with HIS mum, encouraging her to be a bloody hippy almost, wanting him to start paying BOARD money even. Hah, that would be the day! He had been shocked the first time he had walked in and seen her lolling in the armchair, glass of wine in one hand, magazine in the other, there had been no smell of dinner cooking, no table laid in readiness, and when in shocked silence he had finally managed to ask her just what the bloody hell was going on she had said HE, the tosser, had said she should 'put her feet up' once in a while and relax, and as he was the only one in for dinner that night he should 'get some chips' if he wanted. Get some chips! GET SOME CHIPS!! He had blown the roof, and then to add insult to injury, HE, 'the tosser', had come in with fish and chips for just them two. Well . . . the battle that had followed had resulted in him leaving home, no way, no bloody way was he going to live in a house like THAT, be treated like that by his own mother. He had gone straight round to the rest of the family, TOLD them what had happened and they had laughed, each

9

and every one of them laughed. Huh . . . sod them all. If no one else would stay faithful to his dad's memory, HE would.

He looked at his watch, 4.30, he had been here for almost four hours now, oh God, oh God let everything be okay. Please let it be okay, he had that sinking feeling in his stomach right now, and no matter how much he tried to reassure himself it just would not go. Last time he had felt like this had been just after he had left home, things had been tough for a bit, finding somewhere to live and that, he had stayed with a few mates first but they were just as bad, in the end he had got a place of his own, but for a long while that sinking feeling had been with him, he had never considered backing down though, oh no, no way would he admit the tosser and his mum might be right, he would stick it out alone, 'do' for himself. It had made him grow up a lot, and learn a lot too, don't trust ANYONE, sort your OWN problems, rely on no one, be like his dad, tough, strong, yes he would be true to his dad's memory to the end.

And later in the army, he was a private, his regiment was being shipped to Burma – they all knew this was the big one and that most might not be coming back alive; he had been in a state then too, that sinking feeling with him in his gut, it had worried him greatly, think man think, there had to be an answer and he had found it, his sergeant was reputed to be a 'little queer': he would exploit that weakness, because people WERE weak. Look at his mum, his family, his dad had died and they had all fallen apart, gone 'soft' on the discipline that had made order in their lives. He would use their weakness, yes, use it for his own ends.

He aimed all his thoughts at the sergeant, watched him daily, picked up every little scrap of information he could about him, after all 'know thine enemy' the army said, so he said 'hello' in off-duty times when they passed, they were on the ship being transported before things started to pay off. He had almost given up on it, but in the end the pressure of not knowing if you might come back from all this had obviously played on the sergeant's mind too and he had made the move on him. Boy, were his mates envious, ha ha, he would have the last laugh on them, they didn't like him he knew, called him 'creepy Wilson', his sergeant didn't though. He took a shine to him, extra fags, better food, more off-duty time and light duties were within his grasp now he knew. There would be a price to pay, he knew that, but let's face it, ANYTHING was better than dying.

His 'payment' came one evening when after flirting outrageously with him for an hour his sergeant, Ben, suggested they go down and check the inventory together in the hold, he was a bit apprehensive but hey, what the hell, in for a penny eh, and it couldn't be that bad could it? It was, no sooner were they in the hold than Ben had grabbed him, kissed him (the shock from this was terrific) and before he could stop him, had undressed and bent him over a sack of sandbags and done 'THAT' to him. Jesus, Mary and Holy Christ, it had hurt! After that, it was a regular thing, and all the time it happened he had justified it by saying to himself, 'It is worth it, I will stay alive for my wife and my little unborn child'.

He had stayed alive, shunned now not only by his family but the rest of the troops too; he was on his own, with just the sergeant between him and death. It was a long war but he had stayed alive, his comrades fell like flies. He had duties now by his sergeant's side, so was reasonably safe, and when his sergeant had been promoted he had gone with him and been even farther away from danger, the pain was worth it. He had got used to it by now anyway, there was a kind of transience about things around him, bunkers, ditches, tents etc, that made it all temporary and make-do-for-now in his rationality. People put up with discomfort (not the type HE endured, no), they just 'got on' with it.

Yes, he had solved the problem in his own fashion then, had survived the nightmare called war, but now in that hospital his thinking got more erratic, his hands and arms got more taut, he could feel his heart beating away very, very fast. Think, come on think... when you came in the doctors came rushing up to you, perhaps because of the noise she was making, his wife, lying on the trolley, bump in the air oh so pregnant . . . oh God those sounds . . . low, guttural, growling sounds. He remembered hearing those sounds before many years back in the war, hurt sounds all about him, people getting bullets and shrapnel in them, terrible, terrible sounds. Arms and legs blown off . . . guts escaping from chests and stomachs, he had been safe but he had seen others, heard others, that terrible low guttural sound he heard now and also earlier, when he and his pals had cornered a cat, he must have been about 15 or 16 then, so many years ago, and they had decided to experiment on it, please god he hadn't meant to hurt it, and when it started growling those same low guttural sounds he had panicked and killed it, not easily he remembered. it had taken a long time to die, it had struggled and bit, scratched and clawed. It had taken ages to finish it, bashing its skull in with a brick in the end to stop those same sounds. Oh God please forgive me, I promise I will be good for the rest of my life God if only you let things be okay today.

He had buried the cat, him and his mates, and he remembered the old lady it belonged to giving them all sweets to go and search for it and a promise of half a crown to the boy who found it, he knew they wouldn't be getting that. They had talked about it, digging the cat up and taking it to her for the reward, but how could they explain the mutilation and injuries? They had decided in the end to leave it but felt smug, even superior, that something so bad had turned out so good, ha ha ha, and no one would be any the wiser, he thought God was on his side that day and he really had tried to be good after that. But please God . . . please, just this once eh? He had asked before many times and had always found a way then.

The doctors had rushed her off into a room at the side, and he was left there with all this guilt running about inside him. It wasn't his fault really, she shouldn't have talked to him like she did, if his dad had been here he would have given her MUCH worse, it was HER fault. HE was the master of the house, HE earned the money that put food in their bellies, and look what she had done, there was no way he was going to let her get away with what she had done, he would remind her of it daily. If she had listened to him in the first place, let him be in charge like his dad was in their marriage none of this would have happened, it would have been sorted years ago, she ought to be grateful he had stuck by her, not a lot of men would have. He sat down on the empty bench and thought it all over.

She had been an attractive young thing when they met, huh, what had happened to that? It was replaced now by a fat blob, her skin and her looks had gone to the dogs, she didn't take care of herself like she used to, he had shouted and shouted at her to 'buck her ideas up' but to no avail, her hair was always lank, she never wore make-up any more and all the spark had gone out of her. What the hell was wrong with her anyway? He didn't know.

He had taken her out a few times back then and she seemed fine, always laughing, always happy, yes, he had liked her a lot. He always had the feeling she was hiding something inside but outwardly she was bubbly and bright, easy to get on with and popular, that had bothered him a little, he had heard rumours she was a little TOO popular, if you know what he meant, she certainly seemed to need hugs and attention, and the legover, yes, she had kept him off for a while, well not a long while he admitted, but it wasn't the first date, he remembered that. Just a bit of fumbling in the dark the first date, almost there the second, and yes it had been the third date he had her. Okay, it was only three days after their first date but she seemed willing, no resistance, a kind of resignation about it even. Back then he was not so experienced so didn't know if when he entered her he was taking her virginity, afterwards he had learned there should be some resistance, well there certainly hadn't been that! It had slid in nice and easy, easy-peasy in fact, and only later gave more fuel to his suspicions.

And it was nice, nice and easy, she had lain there and let him do it easily, he had enjoyed himself and he didn't have to think too much about her, she seemed okay with it all. And after that it was whenever he wanted, he didn't ask, he just made the move on her and she let him, so surely that was okay? He had heard a few rumours about her, how her sister had a keenness for army men, it was said she flew the flag for her country, had even been with a few darkies, but he held nothing against them, even had a few friends who were black, so what? And the other stuff about her dad, well, he did seem a bit strange as if he knew everything and was somehow in control, but that was nothing, he put it out of his head, it seemed strange that she had to be home by 10, he had walked her home many nights and she had been mighty nervous as she got nearer home. He knew she feared her father, that made him like her even more, she had respect for him or so he thought, that's how women SHOULD be, and sometimes when they were nearly to her place she would cling to him in the dark, want him, come on

13

to him, and they would do it up some entry as if her life depended on it and it was her only joy in life. It made him feel good, she wanted HIM, and he was more than happy to oblige. When they got to hers, then her father would be on the step waiting for them, her and her sisters and would look at them as they passed, examining their faces for a glimpse of guilt, pushing them roughly past him into the house, banishing him with a glance. HA, he had had the last laugh on HIM, if only he had known what had happened five minutes earlier, ha, ha, it didn't bother him anyway, he had a pretty lady who let him do it whenever he wanted, and he was happy.

When he found out she was pregnant he didn't know what to do, he supposed it was his, they were always together so it must have been. Those stories and rumours from others about her being 'loose', well, when had she had the chance, she was either with him or at home and he thought he loved her, they seemed happy enough, he knew the army would be calling on him soon, a war was inevitable and he was the right age to be called up, so marriage seemed a good option, it would give him something to live for, a ready-made family when he got home. It played on his mind a bit that war was dangerous, but he would sort that out somehow and when he did come home he would spit in the eye of his parents and family, ha, he would make his OWN family and THEY would be perfect, just like his dad would have done if he was still alive. He would show everyone. They got married two weeks later.

Two months later he was called up, six months later he received a telegram saying he was the father of a fine healthy son and yes, it helped him through the war, helped him through the pain and humiliation with his sergeant, he had something, something to live for, he had a family and he would make sure for the rest of their lives they knew how lucky they were and how much he had done for them. It was going to be good, it was going to be okay, his contribution to the war was going to be worth it. It would be better if it sounded like he had thrown himself into battle, as they were what he had to live and fight for to make the world a better and safer place for his family … HIS FAMILY … just saying it made him feel stronger. It would all be perfect.

The nurse broke his reverie, she was saying something, what? 'Mr Wilson ... the doctor would like a word with you now, if you don't mind?' Oh God, oh God, what would they say? He hadn't meant to hit her, she just didn't understand, if only she would take the time to listen to him, really listen I mean, not just stand there looking scared, but to try and comprehend what he meant. She was so stupid sometimes, okay she was pregnant, but that just gave her the excuse to be more stupid than normal it seemed.

He followed the nurse to the doctor's office; as he followed he thought again of the past, what had led to all this? It was her, that first leave, coming home to see his wife and his new baby son, the waves of emotion he had felt, love, wanting, and then he had been home, had hugged her in his arms like there was no tomorrow, wanted to have easy, lovely sex with her right that minute and then his baby, wait though, his baby? He looked at the little thing wrapped in the shawl, something was wrong here, this baby was dark-haired and had what looked like a mild suntan, he was fair, very fair, blond even, she saw his questioning look, tried to hide the fear inside herself by saying, 'Doesn't he look like his grand-dad?' And yes, he did, the spit of him in fact, maybe it was genetic. Some people do miss a generation and follow from grandparents, but all those stories and rumours came back to him in an instant and seemed stronger in the thinking. Looked like his granddad? The look from her had given it away, that guilty look, you can't hide something like that, everyone seemed to be fussing around making huge efforts to 'calm' things, and that fuelled the fire even more.

That leave had been terrible, the strain almost unbearable, he almost at one point wanted to go back to war and die there, suffering at the hand of his sergeant preferable to these hidden lies and feelings. She had taken him upstairs almost at once and shagged him senseless, but even that pleasure was tinged with doubt, tainted somehow. She was staying with her parents, so he had come home off leave to them and her dad would not look at him openly, he had challenged him with eyeball contact several times, ready to bring into play his army training and kill if the wrong message was received back, but her dad would not play, looking away instead or playing with his own son, who, by coincidence, was only six months older than the newborn child who now held so much cause for suspicion. In fact, many times he would look into the two prams pushed together, one holding Lawrence, supposedly his, the other Jeff, his wife's young brother, put together they looked more like brothers than nephew and uncle, looking from one to the other then back, thinking, thinking, brooding. Was what he feared to think true? Was his son his or a cuckoo in the nest?

When feeding time came round it was wartime, so breast feeding was the norm, he would look at the babies, one at his mother-in-law's breast-feeding, getting fat off her milk, and the other at his wife's breast, taking milk from HIS wife, HIS ... not someone else's, and a feeling of loathing took him, his wife's breast-feeding someone else's baby, that lovely pap he had suckled on so much, that had given him so much pleasure and now ... and now he could not think too much of it. Cuckolded ... he was cuckolded and then he would look at her dad, his father-in-law, and look for the nearest sign it was true, but would be met with no answers he could confirm.

Worse still, going back to his regiment full of all these feelings, armed with photos of the newborn, the ribbing he took, comments like, 'Milkman Italian, is he?' or 'Feed him a lot of chocolate, then?' The more was said the worse it got, he could see his father-in-law's face in front of him, in his head, olive-skinned, Italian-looking, then the baby next to him laughing up at his daddy? Brewing and brewing inside him, growing like a cancer, and after the war was over whenever he approached the subject, fear and hurt on her face, feeding the hurt in him, she would deny everything, plead her innocence, take him in her arms and let him, no, encourage him, to have her, to quell the beast that rode in his mind with sex. It became a game, a battle almost, he brooded, she gave her body, but how could he respect her after all he had done in the war, all the humiliation, all that pain at the hands of that sergeant, he had done it for THEM ... FOR THEM, for God's sake. She never did say but he knew, he just knew that he was not the father of their supposed son, but he knew, even though it tore him apart inside, he knew who was.

His second son was born two years after the first, and this time all okay, blond and blue-eyed just like his dad. He had made sure of things this time by making a home far across the city from her parents and they only visited once a month or so, and when they did visit she was never alone with her father, he would hover in the background trying to get close to her, to see his son (for he knew it was), he let it be known by showing his new son off to all and sundry, that THIS was his son, the other, well, his son in name but not in truth, but even then he would deny her father the chance of claiming him, HE had to live daily with this thing, HE fed and clothed the child, he would do his duty not from love but because even if he had been cuckolded, no one outside the family would know about it. He could handle the looks, the winks and nods of whispered comments, 'How strange, one is so dark-looking and one is so fair' 'Who do they follow, do you think?' Because he would get his own back eventually he also had a plan to get back to 'normality', he would have a 'pigeon pair', one of each, he had the boy (her second-born) (his first), and next he would have a girl, the eldest boy would be looked after, fed and clothed and such but HIS children would be a pair, a strong healthy son the spit of his dad and a dainty little girl to complement the other. Yes the plan was good, the plan would make things right, the plan HAD to work.

And now it was seven years later, three pregnancies all failed, each one ending the same way. Three chances to make the perfect answer and each time, each and every time something had happened, had she planned it, his wife for some kind of sick revenge for him having her whenever he wanted? Sure she didn't want to sometimes, but there were times when he DID catch her in the right mood, she liked it then all right, responding to his touch, moving with him in sex, why couldn't it be like that every time? But no, she only really got like that when she was pregnant, would go off like a rocket under him sometimes and that fuelled even more hatred, only the babies in her stomach could make her do that, not him. He had her anyway, whether she wanted it or not, it was his right, if she felt ill that was no excuse, she would have to bear it. Two of the unborn children had been girls, if only one had survived, but they hadn't. The other didn't really matter, it had been a boy child, he didn't want one of those, so when he had known it was a boy after she lost it somehow it had been a relief to

17

him. How the hell could his plan work if it was not a girl next? It was a girl he wanted, and each time they tried he would get a little madder, a little more angry, a little more sure that God didn't like him any more. In fact no one liked him, the comments at work worse, much worse than the army gags as soon as they knew how important a daughter was to him, all that stick he got, 'You're not a man, can't make a girl can you?' 'You have to make the opposite to be a man you know', on and on and on, they never let him rest, even when she had lost the girl babies, there was no sympathy. 'Nah, it's not in you, you're just not a man mate', 'Ha, ha, ha, ha, ha, want me to have a go at her? I'll give her a girl all right, I'M a man ha, ha, ha...' on and on they went, never stopping, never giving him a minute's peace, and since one of his old army buddies had joined the factory, it had been worse, stories and innuendoes of that time, of how he had evaded the front line, it had been almost unbearable, but he would win in the end, you wait and see if he didn't.

And now she was pregnant and with TWINS ... how could she? How could she upset his plan, it had to be a GIRL not two, or another boy and a girl, the bigger she got the worse it felt. If they were both born, how could his plan work? It would all be for nothing, oh God. Oh God he hadn't meant to hit her, honestly, it just, well, ended up like that, he had hit her before of course, it was only normal, you had to show them who was boss, his father had shown him that much, let them get out of hand and they ended up like his OWN mother, huh, but this time she had just wound him up and up and up, he TRIED to tell her of the plan but she just talked round it, saying stupid stuff in that silly little girlie voice of hers, God it made him angry, saying it didn't matter what sex the baby was as long as it was healthy, stupid, stupid woman, so he had hit her, what else could he do? It was the same thing when she was pregnant before and he would try to tell her of the plan, reassure her that then things would be different, but she used to say the same thing in that same silly little voice and the tone, the whingeing, stupid, resigned tone in that voice, he had wanted to knock her stupid head off.

And again, this time he tried to tell her what having two would do to their future, how it would ruin the plan, but she just stood there looking stupid and frightened, he hadn't meant to hit her, really he hadn't, but what else could he do? It was just a moment of lost temper, there was no harm in it, but then that sound, oh God, that low growling sob. He had hit her before in the stomach even when she was pregnant but then she had just folded up, sank to the ground in a heap and he had tiraded her with verbal abuse until his temper had gone and then helped her up, told her how sorry he was, wiped the tears from her eyes and cuddled her, they even had sex afterwards usually and she had not complained, lying there beneath him, letting him be master again, it had been good, he had felt in charge. Sometimes she would get cramps after and for a couple of days would be ill, but that did not mean he was responsible for the miscarriages, did it? No one had said it was his fault, but this time it was different: he had hit her full on one side of her bump and she was almost due to drop, he had felt her stomach wince, felt something hard inside beneath his fist and that sound, oh God . . . it was like it came from the bowels of a cavern, oh God, he didn't mean it, honest. Then the neighbours running in from the street when they heard her screams, the panic, the phone call for the ambulance and now this . . . please God, please, please, PLEASE God, let it be all right.

In the antiseptic room he sat and waited for the doctor to finish looking at the X-rays he was holding.

'Your wife is in a lot of pain, Mr Wilson, can you explain what happened?'

He mumbled on about the cat getting caught under her feet, the fall she had from it, how worried he had been . . . all the time he wondered what SHE had said, had she heard the whispered instructions in the ambulance? Her eyes did not give any indication, she had been given a needle straight away by the ambulance-man, the screaming had stopped but the look of pain remained, and he was not sure what she had heard him say, and all the time the doctor just looked at him. He could feel his eyeballs in his head reading the truth, telling him he was speaking lies, but the doctor just said 'Now look here, Mr Wilson, your wife is having twins as you know, we've given her an X-ray and there seems to be some bleeding in her stomach, we're pretty sure one of the babies is all right but we may lose the other.'

'WE MAY LOSE THE OTHER' those words just repeated and repeated in his head, who said there wasn't a God, he had listened after all, the plan would work. Three failures, three attempts at getting it right and now, thanks to him, it WAS going to be all right, it was going to be okay. Oh God, thank you, thank you.

Outside again in the corridor waiting, behind those doors his daughter was going to be born, he knew there was a boy and a girl in there because as she had miscarried before, she had gone for an X-ray a few weeks ago and they had told her then, in fact that had started this latest round of arguments off, he now KNEW there was a girl, they just didn't need the boy that's all. And now, they were giving his wife a caesarean section, cutting his daughter out away from the other, away from the joining with his wife, it would be HIS daughter and let them laugh now, he could walk down the street with HIS son, blond and fine, and HIS daughter, cute and cuddly. If he was careful the other son would be kept out of the way or treated like a cousin just living with them, it was going to work, it was all going to work. Life would be good, he would love his wife, forgive her even, well, he would see, she still had to know who the boss was, of course, but it was going to work out just fine.

There was some noise in the darkness. Time had passed slowly in his hiding sleep, he felt many things, a pulse of something from the joining, drugs? That word was unknown to him, but something had come down from outside and made him very relaxed and drowsy. He felt both his dead twin next to him and an uneasy feeling from the joining, but it didn't matter, only a little of him was awake, the rest was in hiding, safe. He could lie like this for a while, be safe for a bit to think and let things settle, but in one almighty roaring bright burst his world had opened, light, sound, cold, what's happening? What's happening? Faces, smells, rubbing skin, sucking tubes, OUCH . . . a cutting pain in his abdomen, help, help, HELPPP. Hands passing him over, white masks, white gowns, cold touch, crying, screaming, me? Yes, me. Movement out through some doors, calling, calling . . . Another face, not in white this time, a nice face full of love and smiles, holding out arms to take me, looking down at me, ah love. This is not so bad after all. I am safe, the eyes tell me it's okay, don't worry, I have you, I will keep you safe and warm, all with a look instinctive love coming from those eyes down to me, but wait a minute the face is changing. What is this? Horror, disbelief, shock, I don't like this, please love me face. What's happening? What have I done? What's that noise? Is that what's making this love face to hate? What's it saying? Listen ... listen. You listen but you don't yet know language, only the language of your other world, not spoken, felt, from the joining and the other, so you listen to these strange noises and cannot understand what they are saying.

This is the scene then that started my life, a cold hospital corridor, a nurse holding me out at arm's length, a white cloth beneath me to protect her hands from the blood of my birth that covered me, proffered naked, held out for the world to see my gender, and him, looking, looking down on me in disbelief and the words, the words that fill the air, they say; 'Congratulations, Mr Wilson, we couldn't save the girl ... BUT YOU HAVE A FINE HEALTHY SON.'

SIS

I was born on 1 April 1953 and named Alyn Joseph Wilson. As I sit here and write this now, I can't help but think there's some alternative joke in there, as if God's saying; 'Well never mind, life, my old son, it's all one big joke anyway.' April Fool. At the time I didn't think so, in fact, I used to think 'This has GOT to be a joke.'

In short, my childhood was pretty naff. I have been trying to think of some good stuff to put in the early chapters of this story, but I'm afraid I came up short so instead I will tell it as it was, and you can make your own mind up.

History first.

I was born on to a council estate, into a typical council house, modern, quite large, all mod cons for the time, recently built (I believe my family was the first to have moved into the street upon completion, some six months before my birth), having lived in a two-up, two-down cottage before, but with a growing family and my mother's frequent miscarriages it was felt a new house would go a long way to healing her apparent woes. We were lucky in that behind our house there was a large 'allotment' area, and even luckier that we, or should I say they (I wasn't born yet) managed to get the allotment backing on to our house so a simple gate took you right into it from our garden proper.

The people I grew up with were typical working-class people, a local large car factory making up the main source of employment (in fact my father's place of work too), and the factory provided a social club affiliated to CIU for it's employees' enjoyment. The local infant and junior school were adjacent to our street, which also was a cul-de-sac. There was a large 'green' out front for the safe playing area of the street's children, and local shops just around the corner. It was nice, new and very sought-after at the time.

Around the corner from our close was the start of the old council area, and the contrast was startling. One style of house new, modern, 'pretty', met head-on the older style of miner-type concrete terraces, and there were some 'us'/'them' feelings between the areas. Poverty knows no boundaries like those though, and whilst 'that' side of the area suffered very badly from it, 'our' side had its share too.

I have some pretty early memories of my life. I have spoken to people who can't remember before eight or nine years of age but I can remember way before that. The first memory that springs to mind is being out on the green, aged about three, playing with the other children there and my grandfather coming up to me and looking at me funnily, weighing me up almost, he had my Uncle Jeff in his arms (who was about nine then), and I remember vaguely thinking in my young brain that kids his age were not carried round, I wasn't even carried round, and that he must be a very lucky boy. Other memories: arguments between my parents, shouting, crying; good times too: weekend treats like trips to the park, the woods and sometimes my greatest joy, the seaside. And then later at a cousin's birthday party at our house, I don't know why they were there, Sarah (my mum's sister's daughter) was a little older than me by just a few years and I must have been about four.

I remember getting lots of slaps and lots of tellings-off, and learned from an early age to be quiet and keep out of the way if at all possible. My mum was in hospital at the time as she had just had a miscarriage, so that was probably why they were at ours as my aunt and nan used to look after us in the daytime when that happened, while my dad was at work, and now this was just after he had got home and I overheard my dad talking to my uncle about it, just vague stuff, but my attention was drawn to them when they both turned and looked at me and were silent for a second, my ears pricked up to the situation and I heard my dad say, 'I wish HE had died and his sister lived, we wouldn't be going through ANY of this now' ... well, I was flabbergasted. I felt my face going red and I wanted to run away and cry. My mum was in hospital because of

ME? And what else was that – had I killed someone? 'Wished SHE had lived.' Who was SHE?

I think that was the start of it. We went to visit mum in hospital later on that evening and I knew she knew something was up, I couldn't look at her, was I responsible for her being in here? Poor mum, poor, poor mum, and I somehow had done it. After that I learned to listen. About a year later, mum was in hospital again for the same thing, my aunt and grandma had been visiting a lot as mum was in for quite a while, they did the washing and cleaning and that, and it was then that I learned it might not be me but my dad who was to blame for mum. I was only around five but cute with it, I learned to 'be around' when things were being whispered, and had got my ears clipped on more than one occasion for it. I learned that the rows and shouting mum and dad did were NOT part of normal life, and somehow grandma knew all about WHY they were always shouting, but I could never figure out just what it was.

I kept well out of the way whilst mum was in hospital and dad was at home, the looks said it all to me, but on the first Friday she was in, dad went down the club as usual, and I remember being shaken awake in the dark by a very drunk dad, with the next-door neighbour trying to stop him (she was babysitting), and him shouting 'I hate you, you little bastard, I fucking hate you ... why don't you just fucking die and do us all a favour'. I have looked at every key on this keyboard and no matter how I press the keys, or in what order I do it, I just can't find the words to let you see what I felt inside that night.

I guess I could leave a blank space and let you fill in what you would have felt (   ).

Perhaps I can even make you feel a bit better with a small joke. 'What, you need THAT much space?'

Salvation came to some extent in two forms, somebody, somewhere, heard my prayers.

At the age of five or six you aren't very worldly-wise. I was pretty bright though, I learned from almost the year dot that if I buttoned it and looked and listened instead of talking, coupled with learning very rapidly to pick up on other's needs, and what's more, helping them fulfil those needs, then life was a lot easier. I became the 'little gentleman', if you wanted it fetching I got it. Intuition and insight were learned before even words, I could spot a potential situation before I knew what 2 + 2 equalled. I kept as far out of my dad's way as possible, tried not to get in anyone's way, and learned.

One thing I did learn was that my mum was a bit special, well, I suppose ALL mums are special, but I mean she sometimes went a bit 'funny'; let me explain.

We were driving home from an evening out at a country pub one time, it was a nice summer day and we had the caravanette. On the way it was decided to call in for chips at a nice chippy that was usually a bit too far away, but that this time we would be passing quite close. When we got almost there and were waiting to turn right at a junction my mum all of a sudden went a bit funny, she started fidgeting, rubbing her hands together and looked really worried. She told my dad, who was in the middle of the road waiting to turn, to 'go on, don't turn' and became really upset, it was odd, one minute she was okay, the next almost hysterical. There followed a brief row, dad saying how the hell was he NOT to turn now, traffic beeping and swerving as he went straight on instead of turning, and a shouting match followed by silence from mum and dad the rest of the way home. Needless to say, we forewent the chips and were all sent to bed. End of story? No. Blow me down, the very next day on the radio a major smash had happened just a half a mile up the road we would have been on if we had turned, and three people had died in it. Incredibly, we would have been just about where it happened if we had continued the turn. Explain THAT.

Another time, not long after my great-nan had died (much later on than where we are now), mum and nan were in our lounge talking of what had happened to great-nan's wedding ring, as my mum had been looking after it until my nan came to collect it and it now couldn't be found anywhere. They were both in front of the large picture window that faced out our back and I was sat behind them on the sofa, I heard my mum say she knew great-nan would help them find it, when, true as I sit here, it fell out of clear space and 'pinged' to a stop on the tiles in front of them. I could FEEL the hairs on the back of all our necks stand up; there was no explanation, it just fell out of nowhere. I can testify to it as I witnessed the whole thing.

To this day I have no explanation. The doors were shut, windows too, and there were just the three of us in the room. My mum was a bit special all right!

Christmas came early when I was six; in fact it came in September. I had got to the feeling by then that somehow this was all a mistake, there had been a cock-up somewhere in heaven. I had learned by then that I was indeed a twin and that my sister had died shortly before birth. I figured (I was only six, don't forget), that the angels had got the wrong one, like the stork off *Merry Melodies* on TV when it went to the wrong house and Mrs Jumbo got the mouse and vice versa. Well the same had happened to me, simple, they had got the wrong one, I should have died and my twin lived, ha, it was SO easy. So at night I used to go to bed (my two brothers shared the front bedroom, my parents the large back bedroom, and I had the 'wee' room, you know the little room in every house that you put all the junk in). I loved it, I had it all to myself so no one would even be there when the angels came to change things, so every night I would talk to God (because God knew everything), and say, 'Now's your chance, if I go to sleep now,' (because I don't want to know about it, it might hurt) 'YOU can change everything back again, and in the morning no one will be any the wiser.' Good eh? Of course, the downfall of that plan was the feeling of OH, NO, it didn't work, I used to get every time I woke up. I couldn't understand it, I had offered, why didn't it work? And then, the utter resignedness of facing yet another day of living someone else's life, like nicking a chocolate bar and not being able to eat it for fear you would be found out. I had, and was living someone else's life, and it was a living nightmare!

And then salvation (well almost), two things happened in short succession.

My mum went into hospital again, AND GAVE BIRTH TO MY LITTLE BABY SISTER DEE...

And my dad bought a very large fridge...

I remember the day my little sister was born like it was yesterday. My nan and aunt were looking after us again and everybody seemed to be congregating around the kitchen, as that overlooked the road and was where dad would pull up with any news.

We had a motor-caravan at the time, and I remember distinctly everyone running to the front door when it came screaming to a halt outside, its door opening barely before it had stopped, my dad came roaring absolutely maniacally up the pathway, sobbing, shouting, singing, dancing, 'It's a girl! It's a girl!' Everyone was ecstatic, it was like we had won the pools, everyone was jumping up and down, congratulating my dad. All the neighbours were out seeing what all the fuss was about, there was a carnival atmosphere in the square and it was great, everyone was happy, me included, I had a sister. For weeks before I had been keeping a very low profile in case I killed this baby too, but it was all right, she was born, my mum was okay, my dad was happy. I got one look off my dad that time as if to say, 'Hmmm, what am I going to do about you now?' but it passed quickly and I melted into the background out of the way.

That night something else happened.

Dad had come home from visiting my mum and we were all going to bed. My nan had started staying over sometimes by this time, my granddad was ill, and as Jeff my uncle was older, he used to look after my granddad and I think my nan stayed at ours for the break. She used to sleep in my mum's bed with dad, no one thought anything of it in our house, although we were told to say she slept on the sofa because 'the neighbours wouldn't understand'. Understand what I didn't know, but we followed orders. Dad called me over to him and said that as nan wasn't stopping that night I could sleep in his bed with him as a treat and he would tell me a story, well, I was gobsmacked. Was this the difference having a sister meant? It was great. I got into bed with my dad and he asked what story I wanted. I said Tarzan, as that was all the rage on TV at the time and snuggled down next to him and felt, for the first time in my life, warm and loved. He started to recite the story, making it up as he went along and it was great, dad and son stuff, just like off the telly. I was much too excited to go to sleep and I could tell after a bit that he was getting a bit edgy about me not settling down, so I pretended and relaxed, enjoying every minute of this very, very special treat. After a while, he asked if I was awake and I just lay there as if I was asleep and then ... and then ...

I felt the cord on my pyjamas being tugged undone and then my pyjama bottoms pushed down a little. I was by this time concentrating very, very hard not to move and I could feel the hairs on the back of my neck standing up with sheer terror as my treat turned into a nightmare. I felt my dad move very close to me, half lying on his side, me on my back and then some funny movements I didn't recognise at first until I realised he was undoing his own pyjamas and pushing them down, he put his arm under my neck, leant right over me, his belly against my right side, and I felt him playing with himself. With the position we were in he was right next to my willy with his own, he didn't touch me as I half expected, he just put his by now erect penis against mine and started to slowly masturbate himself. He took what seemed like ages, slowing down, speeding up, rubbing it against me, never touching with his hand, just making contact with his manhood. It seemed massive to me even with my eyes shut and concentrating on not moving, hardly breathing, my six-year-old willy seemed minute in comparison to this huge monster of a thing now defiling me. He took ages or what seemed like it and I remember thinking 'Oh no ... oh no ... this is not happening', after everything else in my life, this was the final straw to me and I think that night I gave up, something inside me said, no more hurt, no more, no more, and as he finished what he was doing with a big guttural grunt and sigh, I felt my little private area, the piece of me that was my own secret place receive spurt after spurt of wet sticky jelly, something like that, although I didn't know at the time what it was, I knew beyond all doubt that this was my dad and no matter what happened in my life afterwards now, covered in this sticky, slowly congealing mess, I would always, always be soiled by him and by what had just happened.

I think a little of me died that night. He turned over straight afterwards, I just lay there in the dark, not moving, trying not to think, with this wetness on me covering the most secret place of me and I switched off, nothing was going to hurt me again because I wouldn't feel anything again, no feeling, no hurt, that way I would survive.

The fridge? Well, that really was a godsend. Dad bought this monstrously big old-fashioned fridge, real 1950s style, rounded top and with a handle you had to pull out to actually open the door. The way our kitchen was designed meant that the only place it would fit was beside the old larder, a concrete affair that sat in the corner of the kitchen. We had a big crock sink and an old-fashioned wooden drainer attached to it, then the fridge next to that, which left a gap absolutely and perfectly big enough for me to slide into. I could spend hours and hours in the gap, hardly being noticed, but being able to be 'part' of things as well. I was there but not there, if you know what I mean. I suppose it became my bolt-hole in a way, I always felt slightly excluded from family life as if I wasn't quite part of it all, but here, tucked away up the corner of the kitchen unobserved, almost invisible as part of the furniture, I could at least watch my world from a distance.

Looking back, I suppose I did become a bit of a spy. Any of you with children will recognise that children have big ears, and how many times have you been talking about something and realised that every word you say is being digested by small ears, who obviously are picking their way through a conversation you just KNOW they are going to ask awkward questions about later. So I found myself a few times being ejected from my hidey-hole with a cuffed ear, but on the whole I learned an awful lot.

If I can diverge here for a minute, it took me an awfully long time to finish this last bit. There seem to be two very separate and distinct sections of giving an account of my upbringing. One is the words, you open your mouth, form your lips and tongue, exhale air in a certain way and words come from your mouth, these words tell the story, 'nuff said. Likewise, I sit here and press certain keys on the keyboard, again forming words, and the story unfolds.

There is another side to all of this, and it's something I still have difficulty coming to terms with, feelings. For every expression I write there is connected to it a feeling. I write, 'I stood in a gap alongside the fridge', it doesn't sound much, does it? What that means is, me, a person, in the kitchen living every day as part of a family, moving about in a house shared with five others and standing day after day in a gap about 1 foot 6 inches by 2 foot 6 inches, lodged in the corner of the kitchen between a cold wall and the side of an old fridge, being part of a group of people whose lives are carrying on day to day as normal, but there being an invisible, almost intangible barrier, like a glass wall, between them and me. I watched everyday events, things you wouldn't think twice about normally happening every day, and somehow I wasn't part of it all. I was watching it all from the other side of existence, in a little gap by the fridge, my emotions switched well and truly off, accepting everything as 'Well, this is or must be how things are' and wanting so much to be 'normal'.

Since that night with my dad I had become a total blank but now, writing the words, making the past come to life on this paper, every word I write hurts. Standing by the fridge therefore becomes overwhelming loneliness, a feeling of being worth nothing because if I were worth something I would have been out there amongst the others, part of things.

Lying in bed with my dad that night – eight little words. What that means is a complete and utter feeling of disgust, of worthlessness, of dirtiness. Your soul can only dip so far down, and that night mine was at the very bottom of a dark, black pit. I think we have all at one time or another had the feeling we wished the earth would open up and take us from the moment. Well, magnify that to infinity, and all in a little boy of six.

At that time in my life I didn't exist. I was a nothing, a dirty, horrible, unwanted little nothing.

I can write the words because words are just words. I can skip over the dad/bed thing and go on to the fridge thing because that way it is written quickly, but those few lines, that hour or so of my life, sticks in my head like a pikestaff. Even when now I look at it with a half-glance of thought, it fills me with pain.

There is perhaps one other incident I could put in here to help give the flavour of the time.

We always had plenty of fruit and salad in our house; we had a small piece of land at the back and vegetables, fruit and salad stuff were always available. My diet, I must say, was always a healthy one, dad used to grow tomatoes and cucumbers in the greenhouse and I developed a liking when mum cut the cucumber up for the bit left over, you know, the bit that originally joined it to the plant, and my mum over time noticed this and as a treat would leave a little bit of the cucumber on the end and give it to me. I used to sit quite happily munching on this small treat and think I was in heaven, my mum had given me a treat, it was great.

One day dad noticed her giving me this and asked why so much had been left on and not put in the salad we were having that night, there was a bit of a row about it in fact, and I disappeared out onto the front step out of the way to nibble my treat. There was a window in the bedroom directly above the front step and a little while later I heard it open, I didn't think much of it at the time, it was a warm summer's day and the windows would normally be opened. I, anyway, was busy watching the world go by, quite happy in my moment.

My dad had a disgusting habit of snorting and spitting, if you know what I mean, handkerchiefs were NOT used by him, and many times I can remember heaving quietly when he did this, to me, quite horrible thing.

I vaguely heard him in the background doing it, but switched my ears off to it as I was eating, I had just got to that interesting stage of nibbling the skin off the outside of the cucumber and now had the lovely fleshy inside left to eat, yum. I know it sounds silly now, but we all have our foibles and that at the time was mine. To this day I still sit and ponder whether it was pure fluke or a deliberate act but, yes, you have probably already guessed, a second later a large lumpy dollop of spit, snot and ugliness came down from above and landed right on top of my treat. I looked up quickly and dad was looking down on me, laughing his head off. I just sat there, I was so humiliated. I just sat there for what seemed like ages with this ... this ... mess all over me. I couldn't look at it, I would have been sick, so I just ignored it and sat looking out at the world as if nothing had happened. Mum came out a little later and told me off for not eating what she had just had a row about giving me; I put the object in the bin, washed my hands and never ate cucumber for a very, very, very long time. That was my dad.

Phew ... after writing the last bit I found myself crying again; bringing back such memories is quite painful for me.

I went up to the crematorium and stood at the place my parent's ashes are scattered and asked them why. Why had they let it happen? I was just a little boy, why didn't they love me for that? I had the feeling they were both standing right there next to me, and that finally I had my parents with me and that they loved me and were saying it would be all right. That in heaven they now understood that it had been an earthly mistake, that when I got up there I would be okay too.

It lasted for a few minutes. I guess there is no basis for believing it, but it was nice for a minute to feel loved.

I guess every little boy needs to be loved, and sometimes I feel the little boy in me crying out for just that.

I know from experience how hard it is to be a parent, I have made my share of wrongdoings in that direction myself with my own children. I hope they know how much I love them.

FIRST CONTACT

'Oh yes, I remember it well.' A bit like the song, I do remember it well, my first sexual experience.

I was approaching the age of eight, keeping my head down, and getting through life.

One Sunday we had visitors, my uncle and aunt came over. They had five children who roughly mirrored our family, one of their daughters was called Sarah and it was her sixteenth birthday, she was a bit annoyed to be at our place as, being her birthday, I guess she wanted to be with her own friends and not stuck with a load of grown-ups. However, she cheered up when she realised that my two brothers had their friends around, as well as my older uncle, and so she had company of her own age and my uncle who was 19 at the time.

At first she didn't want to stay at all but quickly changed her mind, and when my uncle and aunt wanted to go persuaded them to leave her behind and pick her up later for a family tea that had been organised. This done, I noticed (hovering in the background as I was) that an awful lot of flirting was going on and Sarah was obviously enjoying being centre of attention. There were at this time my older brothers, aged 17 and 19, one of their friends aged about the same, and my Uncle Jeff (he was to play a large part in my life later on, but at this time I just knew him as 'Uncle Jeff'). Anyhow, there seemed to be a big effort to get Sarah away from the rest of the family, and I could clearly see little plots and schemes going on to achieve this. Obviously, to the annoyance of my brothers as I was just a baby, and much too young to be involved with grown-up matters, I pestered and pried around the edge of them until my eldest brother complained to my mum who said, 'For God's sake, he's doing no harm, why don't you all go up the patch (the large area at the rear of our garden housing a shed and a vegetable garden) and take him with you, he is your brother.'

Quick glances were exchanged, which only intrigued me more, and it was agreed on the condition I kept out the way as much as possible. So, all six of us made for the patch, and when there made a beeline for the shed. I was last in and so was told to 'keep watch' as they were going to help Sarah celebrate her birthday properly. I had no idea what they were on about, but this was all strange and new stuff and I was totally fascinated by everything that was going on. I knew I was there under sufferance, but this was big boy stuff and I didn't want to miss a second of it.

The shed was about ten by eight with windows along one side and a door on the end, pretty basic inside, no shelves or anything and, apart from the lawnmower and spade and fork in one corner, empty. The atmosphere though was electric, and amongst the giggling and comments being passed between the lads I had a fair idea that something slightly naughty was afoot. Lawrence, my older brother, had by this time cornered Sarah at the back of the shed and was kissing and cuddling her, much to the delight of the rest present. From where I was at the end of the shed I had a pretty good view of things as the rest were lining up along the window to hide what was going on from the outside, although with six of us in there it was a bit cramped. More giggling, and I watched wide-eyed as Lawrence undid Sarah's blouse, I could see her lacy bra underneath (the first one I'd ever seen), and then after taking off her blouse completely he reached behind her, did something and ... her bra came away from her body, showing her firm young breasts to us all. Well, the atmosphere went from electric to ecstatic, it went quite silent after that as we all looked on as Lawrence instigated events by taking one of her breasts in his hand and fondling it, before bending slightly and taking it in his mouth and suckling on her.

I remember feeling stuff I had never felt before, a kind of rush and slight dizziness as if all this was not really going on, but it was and right in front of my eyes. Lawrence continued fondling and kissing her breasts, moving from one to the other as he pleased, I could see Sarah was enjoying it, she too seemed to be having a rush, or at least that's what it looked like, the way her body was moving and responding to his touch. As all this was happening in mid-June it was pretty hot and the general mode of dress was jeans and tee-shirts for the boys, and Sarah, now naked from the waist up, had on just a short skirt, white socks and trainers. Lawrence by now was well into it all, looking around at his counterparts with a look like the cat that had the cream. Taking my eyes off Sarah for a minute, I could see the rest had their hands in their pockets and were obviously playing with themselves (something I had recently learned to do myself), and Danny, my brother's other friend, had taken his erect penis out and was openly playing with himself. At my age and as it was my first sexual experience, it looked absolutely ENORMOUS and must have been about 8/9 inches long, hell, compared to my young 3/4 inches it WAS enormous and thick with it.

Danny doing that seemed to stir things on as Uncle Jeff said, 'For God's sake, Loz, get on with it or we'll all come in our pants.' All this strange talk. Lawrence grinned and then, oh no, I couldn't believe it, he started to lift Sarah's skirt up then, thinking twice about it, he told her to turn around, he then undid her skirt at the back and it slid to the floor where she stooped and picked it up, hanging it with her by now discarded blouse over the handle of the mower. She was left with just a pair of brief white panties on, and I looked round at the others to see if they were as dumbfounded as I was at all this. My two brothers and Uncle Jeff had now taken their erect penises out and to my eyes, looking as I was from the end of the line, I was confronted with a line of throbbing male members the likes and size of which I had never even imagined, let alone seen before, each one being teased and touched by its owner and looking to all intents and purposes as if they were about to explode. I could actually make out one or two throbbing in time with the heartbeats that were by now threatening to explode my own heart in my body.

I took a second to think of my own feelings and realised I too had a raging erection. Feeling a little inferior to the monsters lined up in front of me, though, I did not take mine out but contented myself with feeling it through my shorts pocket (thank you mum for buying me baggy shorts). I glanced up at the faces of the others and they seemed to be in some kind of trance, their eyes were glazed-looking and all attention was fixed firmly on Sarah and what was unfolding before us in the corner. I looked back to Sarah and nearly fainted, she had taken Lawrence's penis out and was now playing with it, he on the other hand had got his hand down her panties, sliding them down slightly in doing so and I could clearly see there before me my first sight of a female fanny. Lawrence's fingers were sliding in and out of her, touching her all over that area (I didn't even have a name for what I was seeing right now). She had wispy, quite thin blonde hair down there, and it was only then I associated, oh yeah, the hair on your head was the same as that on other parts of your body, but only for a second as it was all happening in the corner by now. Loz had taken off her panties altogether and they now lay on top of her other clothes on the mower, his own jeans and underwear were now round his ankles, and I watched in stunned excitement as he manoeuvred her against the back wall of the shed and stood in front of her.

Picture this scene . . . a shed, me at the end by the door, look left; a row of three erect throbbing penises the owners of which all had their jeans round their ankles too, tee-shirts off, so semi-naked, lined up, almost steaming from the ears – and look right; a naked (apart from socks and trainers) 16-year-old, spreadeagled against the wall with another semi-naked youth standing against her doing whh. . . att. . . I didn't believe my eyes. I had to blink to make sure I was awake. Lawrence bent his knees slightly, took his what seemed like a monstrous prick in his hand and Sarah, opening her legs somewhat, proceeded to feel, then rub, then push his huge stiffness slowly into her. I couldn't believe it. I just couldn't believe it, and at this moment I realised I had stopped breathing for a minute, I took a few deep breaths and watched. Watched bloody absorbed at perfect eye level to me, not more than a few feet away, Lawrence slowly going in and out of her, each time he withdrew I could clearly see his penis coated in liquid, sheathed in her/his juices, as he slowly fucked her in front of me, she lay slightly back, pushing her pelvis forward to him. It must have only been a few minutes but it felt like hours as he took her, helping himself to a suck on her breasts now and then, getting slowly faster and more urgent until with her moaning slightly and him breathing fast he seemed to groan, explode and shudder all at the same time, leaning into her as he did so, his eyes half shut and almost a look of pain on his face. My head was pounding, my heart was racing and I could barely stand up straight from the lightheaded feeling I had, and I watched. Lawrence after a few seconds seemed to recover himself, stood up and away, and his cock slipped with a plop sound from her. As he turned away I could see the monster hanging there, still semi-erect, coated with slime? Drips of which hung from the end and seemingly to steam. A glance at Sarah showed, for a second, blobs of the gooey stuff on her hair down there, to be hidden by oh God ... oh God ... Mickey, my older brother, now taking up position where Lawrence had left off.

A trance, this was a trance, a dream, I would wake up in a minute I was sure, my eyes were glued to the action. I watched, overawed as Mickey, then Danny, then Jeff, repeated what Lawrence had done, each one getting hotter, more urgent, with a sense of 'raw', 'primeval' caveman about it. With one difference – when Jeff took his turn there was something about it – a managed kind of 'I'm in charge and I orchestrated it' feel to things, as if this was what HE had wanted. I hadn't noticed before (I had been too engrossed in the action in front of me), but as he took his turn, it was just that he TOOK her, the others had done it with her, he took her, used her, even I at my young age felt that as he slid in and out. He seemed to get heightened pleasure from the fact he was last in line instead of first and another thing, more worrying in fact, whilst he had her he did not look at her but at the others who he had asked to remain undressed in case they wanted 'seconds' he had said, but I had the feeling he just wanted to see their willies as he was now moving in and out of Sarah but looking at the others playing with their semi-hard-ons and his eyes gave away some- thing, something frightening he looked at me too, and it made me shiver inside.

He took the longest, being the oldest. I had the feeling he had done it many times before, whether with Sarah or not I don't know, but he took his pleasure now and when he neared his climax it was as if there was a mist in the shed as if all became so intense it clouded not only your brain and vision but almost the air too. He

37

came with a great low moan. Oooooh, I looked at Sarah, she tolerated it I could tell, he had some kind of power over her it was obvious, he also had by far the larger member and when eventually he slid from her, whether from the mixture of four different deposits or him producing so much, a long sticky 'thread' of sperm still connected them for an instance and when broken hung like a wet spider web from his manhood (and her inner thigh it must be said), something else not acted on, just picked up by me (and the others?), as if he wanted more but not the same, I didn't know then what (but I would find out one day).

Me. I had stood as if dazed and watched the last hour in fascination. It seemed to be winding down – the others, after Jeff had finished, seemed to have picked up the same message I had and were all turning away as if not to go there, so it looked as if 'seconds' were not going to happen. I knew with pounding heart that if I didn't do something now the moment would pass. With hardly any breath and little hope of succeeding I spoke, 'What about me?' Everyone turned to me and from their faces I knew I would be laughed at, but not Jeff, he said something like, 'Better let him, if he does it too, he is as guilty as us and can't snitch.' There was some objection from Sarah, who in retrospect must have been quite sore by then, but after a look and some mumbling from Jeff to her, acquiesced. So she again took her position against the wall, opened her legs and waited.

To this day I don't know how I moved the eight to ten feet across that shed, I got in front of her, I took out my own penis, stiff as an iron bar, but far, far smaller than had been on show. The others by this time were getting dressed, pulling clothes back on or up, so paid little or no attention. Jeff however did, as I moved forward he looked over my shoulder and down at me, looked and saw and smiled. I was too overcome with the situation to log that look properly, I moved closer to Sarah, touched for the first time a woman's part, hot, wet, slippery, I fumbled about not knowing what I was doing or where I was going, rubbing me against her.

Another two things happened in short succession, Jeff moved his hand over between us, Sarah and I, and, touching me, pointed me in the right direction, all at once I slid into her. Words, words to describe that feeling – there are no words sufficient to describe it. I slid in, my foreskin sliding back for the first time, my skin against her skin, mine so tender and young and new, hard and hot, hers so soft, wet, used, full of the stuff of the others. I slid in AND CAME. My first orgasm. I had played with myself before in the safe confines of my bed in the dark, I had experimented with those warm funny feelings when you rubbed yourself, gone to sleep feeling excited and exhilarated by it all, but this was different, if that was Christmas this was fireworks and flying to the moon and ... and well, a warm, explosive, tingly, all-over drugged euphoria that was like nothing I had ever felt before. That feeling afterwards, too. Satisfaction, complete and sheer satisfaction from your toes to your fingertips, and every bit in between, your head so far away from this world you could be in heaven. All this in a few moments then, and when after just a few moments real time (but a lifetime orgasm time), I reclaimed reality. I realised Jeff's hand was still there, feeling, smiling down at me with those eyes. I made to move away and the second thing happened, almost another explosion.

The rest were by now dressed, Sarah still naked apart from bobby socks and pumps, me with my willy out and dripping sticky stuff, and the shed door burst open and my dad stood there with Sarah's dad. Horror! Shouting, swearing, the boys scattering under a wave of blows from her dad to anyone in the way, me, standing there like an idiot, the proverbial turkey head from the butcher's shop hanging from my shorts top (they were round my knees), Sarah as red in the face as between her legs and me in total euphoria. They could have declared World War Three and I would not have cared.

The rest of the day (and a few after) are a bit of a blur, shouting (seemed like everyone), me sent to my room, people crying, how the police weren't called I don't know. The upshot of it was, I later learned, it was said (by Jeff) that Sarah had got excited, it being her birthday, it was a hot June day, they had wanted to experiment but that she was not sure, so had tried it with me being the youngest and smallest to see if it hurt etc., and that I had been the first and no one else had done anything.

Maths, never my strong point, but getting around what felt like a pint of sperm from testicles that could hold at that time no more than an ounce confuses me. How it was explained away I don't know, perhaps they didn't look.

The others were warned, threatened, scolded. Sarah was incommunicado for some time. Me, I didn't give a fig, I wasn't part of life anyway, and I had a memory that would last a lifetime.

ROAD TO HELL

Have you ever watched a horror movie, knowing that feeling of fear mixed with excitement? Knowing it's not right, but being drawn to it for whatever reason?

I was drawn to Jeff.

I feared him greatly but he showed me kindness, well, at least in the beginning. Since that day in the shed he had made extra special efforts to be near me. Whenever we visited 'nan' he would always have a friendly word or hug. I guess people thought it was to make up for him supposedly letting what happened in the shed happen, and he was simply now 'putting things right' with extra thought, care and love for me. I knew what they thought had happened in the shed was complete lies, so in a way I had one over on Jeff, he 'owed' me, and that justified in me letting him spoil me a bit. I had taken the blame, so now I was getting the payback. Good, I thought.

I always got on well with my nan, I think a little to do with the time I was smaller. I couldn't pronounce 'Alyn', it came out 'Nanin', hence my nickname. From an early age no one called me anything but 'Nanin' or 'Nantan', so the similarity to 'nan' from my nickname made some kind of link to my gran.

When visiting, it was said, 'Let's take Nantan to see his nan then' or suchlike, and when we got there it was 'Nan, your name-sake's here', etc., so me and nan got on pretty well. Also, I remembered the times in the past when she had come to look after us whilst mum was in hospital, she was one of the few people that treated me okay, and I used to remember getting 'that look' from her as if to say, 'Yes, I understand you little man'. I loved my nan (I suppose that's what nans are for) – I loved my mum too, but

41

differently. I always feared that if my mum was seen to love me too much my dad would get to know and punish us both, silly isn't it, what goes through a child's mind sometimes? But nan was different, removed somehow from my home-life proper. Also, she seemed to have an affinity with my dad that my mum didn't have, some kind of power over him. As I got older it got a bit embarrassing to be called by such a silly name, but it was a family thing, accepted, and I just got on with it. Truth be known, I had a feeling deep down it was one of my father's ways of subtly keeping me 'down'. Who could think anything of a person called Nanin? But to me I had a silent small victory over him, as far from doing what he thought, I secretly LIKED the fact I had a special name. It made me different, and as my self worth was nil anyway (I felt I was a non-person from that day Dee was born), I thought 'Pooh to you dad!'

One particular incident springs to mind when we were away on a family holiday in Cornwall – my mum, dad, Dee and me. We were in the back of a real old-fashioned Cornish pub and a local rugby team had just descended on the place after a match. It was packed in there, and being tucked away in the corner as we were made it even more intimidating. I was about 13 at the time and feeling in the way, as I had been staying at my nan's for the past month and had only gone home for the reason of this holiday, but felt uncomfortable being cooped up with dad for so long a time in so confined a space. My dad went up to the bar to get another drink and shouted right down the room, 'NANIN, DO YOU WANT POP AGAIN OR A SHANDY LIKE YOUR MUM'S?' All eyes looked my way – was Nanin a boy, a girl or what? Again, my dad stood at the bar with a sick grin on his face. That was my dad.

I liked the attention I got from Jeff anyway, he made me feel what I knew I wasn't, namely special. I used to start staying at my nan's at every opportunity, it was lots better than home, at least I didn't have to hide there, and as Jeff was by then 20 (when I started staying over), and me nine-ish, he was more like my older brother than an uncle.

When I started staying over, nan was having some alterations done to her house, a bathroom and roof repairs, so we all used to sleep on the lounge floor in one giant bed, it was fab, like camping

42

out, all snuggled up together. By then Sarah was living at nan's, I think after the shed incident she and her dad didn't get on (a bit like me in fact), so when my nan offered to take her in no one argued. I secretly used to hope I too could live there permanently, but I guess one extra mouth on a permanent basis was enough as my granddad had by this time died of consumption. It was nice though, I was happy. Yes, happy.

The regime for bedtime was everyone took turns in the kitchen to wash in a big old tin bath, nan, then Sarah, then Jeff, then me. Jeff used to stand watch over me in case I 'burned' myself or anything, this big, strong person caring for me, watching my every move, sometimes moving to hold me if he thought I was about to fall in the slippery bath, telling me to 'wash that bit' if he thought I had missed somewhere. I grew quite used to him and being in the company of him whilst semi or completely undressed. It was 'normal, natural'. Sometimes he used to call me in the kitchen for my bath whilst he was still getting dried, to 'save the water getting too cold', and as I undressed he would be drying himself with a big fluffy towel (my nan had the fluffiest towels and bed sheets I ever knew), and his body would be there, naked, and I used to look at him as he did me, his what seemed like a huge penis hanging there, semi-hard, and it reminded me of the things in the shed. Thinking of the 'sex' thing, remembering how Sarah felt, wet and warm, and I had a funny warm feeling myself from it. After all, Jeff and I had shared the same feeling, we were 'pals', related friends. It was 'nice', 'safe' and 'warm'.

Into bed then, one large bed made up of blankets (no quilts in those days) underneath, then sheets (oh so soft) and more blankets on top. The line-up was Sarah, then nan, then Jeff, then me, and as the roof wasn't on properly we all used to snuggle up in the warm with a real coal fire going (on my side), and it felt lovely. Jeff would turn into me and we would make 'spoons' together. I felt so protected and nice. I think those nights were the best times of my life up until then. I used to fantasise about Jeff being my dad and my nan being my mum and I lived here with them with Sarah as my sister; everything would have been rosy red and lovely, we would be a family, a proper family, and each day I would be loved. I wanted them to go on forever.

43

Sometimes not long after we had gone to bed I would feel something hard in the small of my back and Jeff would make a noise or movement to say he was a little uncomfortable, he was always careful not to disturb nan, and I guess I knew in the back of my thoughts what the lump was. I used to get erections myself by then, ha, almost constantly it seemed (much to my embarrassment), and I, in my naïvety, would wonder what I could do to repay this kind, wonderful man to make him comfortable, but knew not what would do it, so would snuggle in closer and let him know that I cared about him too, that I shared the feeling with him, knew what he felt, we were like members of a secret gang with a membership of two. We were special. Sometimes our jamas (we all wore nightclothes, it was all very respectable) would be soaking early in the night as the fire and body temperature mixed together and the blankets were thrown off us all, then later, when the fire was out and it got cold, me being on the fire side and feeling the draught from the chimney, would wake and pull the blankets back over our side, Jeff and myself, and I would look at this person who cared for me in the half light of morning, peaceful in his sleep, so strong and big, protective, and love him a little for loving me.

So, the repairs complete, we all moved back upstairs. There used to be three bedrooms, but one had been turned into a bathroom (I think gran used the money from granddad's death for the alterations). So nan and Sarah slept in the back big room and Jeff in the front; he had a large double bed (the others had two singles), and when I stayed I used to sleep with him in it.

At first it was brilliant, it felt even more special, our own secret place, just us, private, like a den, 'boys' own' stuff. I was out of the way of my family, they were happy. I was in an environment of caring and I had someone to look after me, it was great. Again it was summer, so we 'dared' to dispense with jamas and slept in just pants, oh, the excitement! Me, nine years old, almost naked in a big bed, our 'den,' with my big brother uncle. Oh, what a naïve plonker I was.

Since that day in the shed I had masturbated frequently. In fact, my mum had embarrassed me mightily one day from my hidey-hole beside the fridge when she commented on the 'white marks' on my sheets. After that I made sure I had toilet tissue to hand at night as I had found something that not only gave me GREAT pleasure, it didn't cost anything or involve anyone else either, and the visions of the 'shed day' would keep me in motivation for a very long time (to this day even). So I knew about sex and those feelings. Also, the estate I grew up on was rife with sex, each day at school even, I would hear tales from the other lads of who 'did' it and who didn't. Looking back, I know I was a wholly normal, heterosexual little boy at that time; women, the female form, 'tits' and the like absorbed me, sexual stimulation, however, came from the only source I had yet encountered, the 'shed day', so the male form was in there somewhere too. It was like being broken in to sex on a background of voyeurism and live blue movies, but at the age of nine things were a little mixed up still. I had awakening feelings, hormonal changes going on at breakneck speed, and an overwhelming need to fulfil those urges. I hid the feelings I had about the negative side of the day, the manipulation, the touching of me, and that look in Jeff's eyes that had frightened me deep down inside; after all I had someone who wanted and liked me – I wasn't about to endanger that. Looking back, having read books on paedophilia since, the subtlety of the whole thing was very, very conniving; the road I took to hell at this person's hand was not very well signposted to me but known like the back of his hand to him.

It started this way.

All the signals I had been given whilst sharing the communal bed were now transferred to our bed, but we had less clothes on and no one there to notice. I was sexually immature but very, very keen to explore this new-found euphoria-inducing act, anything remotely sexual, forbidden or secret got me going. Imagine the excitement, then, one night when it was suggested we sleep 'in the buff'. Wow! The though of us naked, daring! We even left the curtains open that night (the only thing that could have seen us would have been a passing spaceship, but that didn't matter then as the illegality of it all, the half threat of someone seeing us was very erotic). Wow. We threw back the bedclothes, lying there together in the moonlight, cool breeze from the window, hot night, boy did it feel good. I certainly had a stiffy from it all, and Jeff noticed it. There was various talk: 'Look at that, you certainly like this don't you, it feels nice eh?' touching ourselves, watching each other touch ourselves. It was all right, we had bathed in the same room, shared experiences of that nature, it was safe, okay, nice. What harm could it do? It felt oh so good him touching me.

I don't remember the exact moment it just happened, then him saying I should touch him, me doing it, thinking that big thing had Sarah that day. I remembered what it looked like, how I had felt, I wanted that feeling again, for me. I wanted to be big and powerful and in charge. I wanted to be able to 'do' stuff like a grown-up and not have to ask. I touched, played, he with me, how was this wrong? It was SO nice. It progressed, we played, rubbed, vague memories of what my dad had done crept into my head, I pushed them out. This was not bad, not horrible like that night, this was clean, nice, we were doing it together, not being forced or made to do it, it was by mutual consent, we CARED for each other – and something else, like the horror film, I, yes ME, I could do it now, I knew it was wrong but I was in control, or so I thought. Jeff let me do what I wanted and in return did what he wanted with me, it became a secret pact between us, OUR secret, our special thing.

It progressed, we used to masturbate each other openly, bed-clothes thrown back, free to the world, he knew exactly what to do to 'get me off'. I learned loads of stuff, how to get satisfaction the best way, how and when to do what and how to attain maximum pleasure. He taught me what to do for him, watching him spurt his stuff over my hand, his body. I used to think 'How can something the same be so bad one time (with my dad), and so nice now?' It was electric. I was exploring, I wanted to do all that with a grown-up body like his, with Sarah, to repeat what he had done myself, but for now I was satisfied. I was not fully developed, and in look-ing back know that I was quite large for my age and have since developed perfectly into a complete sexual form. At that time, however, I looked so small against him and wanted so desperately to be like him.

When I came at his hand he would move a little closer and give a small moan, letting me know how nice it was for him too in satisfying me and making it even more special. I used to wonder if Sarah would do that or if any woman would be the same as this.

Then one time he paid special attention to me, took a long time in pleasuring me, and as I came he moved his head close and took me in his mouth. Oh God it was nice! I knew it was wrong, every brain cell said so, but it was SO like going into Sarah that time, warm and wet and nice. I closed my eyes and let it happen, shut out the guilt, shut out that it was a male and not a female as I wanted, I was an expert at shutting things out, don't forget.

Payback? Yes, you guessed it. I lay there in the aftermath of this emotional explosion, he sat half up, his own erection throbbing, I could see it pulsing in the half light, wanting, urging, needing release. I looked at him, his expression said it all without him saying a word, he wanted that too, that release, that feeling he had just given me. He had given; I owed him. Things changed that night, my nightmare began. I leant over, he grabbed my head, held me close, hard, forcefully, and did without my full permission what he had done to Sarah that day, no gentle masturbation, no kindness, no thought of me or my feelings, he took me, took my mouth and forced himself into me until I could hardly breathe, his hand on the back of my head, half leaning, half laying, he pushed my face onto his giant erection, thrusting with every stab, gagging me, my blood beating loudly in my veins, my head thudding at the suddenness, the ferocity of it, then he came. No warning, just floods of it, filling my mouth, choking my throat. I swallowed, choked, there was loads of it forced into me, no chance to say if I wanted it or not, no choice, just what seemed like pints of hot, smelly sperm in my mouth, in my body, swallowed.

I will never forget the smell and taste of that time, the retching feeling inside, the trying to swallow, breathe even. As I struggled to cope with things, I felt sick but switched it off, I felt faint but numbness took over. I did what I knew best – I stopped feeling. I didn't think there was much of me left after my past, but I died a little bit more that night.

He rolled straight over when he'd finished and went to sleep, I think. I didn't really know. I was back there in the same place I was with my dad that night, used, dirty, disgusted, both with the situation and for letting it happen, but it was too late then, wasn't it? My private parts had been used before on that night with dad, he had dirtied them forever, sullied them with his stuff, and now my mouth too and my insides. I had swallowed it – it was in me! Both outside and inside of me, where, where . . . Nowhere on this keyboard are the letters or words to describe that feeling. I was less than nothing, I lay there with the taste of that stuff in my mouth, trying not to retch, feeling it in my stomach like eating a bad food item and knowing it will come back up if I didn't concentrate hard, thinking to myself, stupidly enough, that my nan would go mad if I was sick on her soft sheets, ha, what an innocent I was and just desperately trying not to feel any feelings because I knew if I complained, or said anything, they would not love me any more and I would be alone again.

I know now there are some of you out there who have also felt that feeling. My heart goes out to you as you read this – know, KNOW, that I am with you for an instant in time. I am with you, we are kindred spirits. You are not alone.

But on that night a very frightened, shocked little boy called Nanin was.

FOLLOW THE PATH

I was nine when it started, I was sixteen when it stopped, and in the in-between years I followed the path life set for me.

I spent more time at my nan's, when I went to senior, or upper school as it is now called; it was just round the corner from nan's and five odd miles away from my house, so it was logical to stay at nan's a lot.

That suited Jeff great. By this time I had given up, thoughts of ever leading a 'normal' life were gone and forgotten. From an early age I had learned if I pleased people I would be liked for it, so pleasing Jeff was no different. I was dirty, degraded, the trick was just not to think of it, lock it out of my life. That night with dad I learned if you didn't feel, it couldn't hurt you. That first night with Jeff just confirmed it. I still had feelings, so I just got what satisfaction I could from life and accepted my fate.

The abuse became worse, much worse. What happened that night became a regular thing. If my sexual needs were seen to as well it was a bonus, but mostly it was just his needs, there was no going back now, I could not 'undo' what had happened. I was dirty, contaminated, no one would ever want me, so I just let things carry on.

My parents, go to them, ha, ha. I was, to them it seemed, well taken care of, out of the way. Dad was happy: he had Mickey and Dee, his pigeon pair. Lawrence by this time was off living with his girlfriend. Mum was happy, there was reasonable peace in the marital home, and so it wasn't an option to tell them. I did try once. One Friday after school, Jeff had taken me to a park; there was something going on, I could feel it, he was working by this time and we were supposedly meeting one of his pals there. We

49

did, and as he approached he looked at me and said to Jeff, 'You're right, nice isn't he, and so young.' The pal was a big fat man of about 40, there was some discussion in mumbles between them, money changed hands and I was forcibly led round the back of a snooker pavilion by Jeff and told to 'Do as he tells you or I'll bash you.' Doing as he told me turned out to be his pal leaning up against the snooker hall wall and dropping his trousers whilst I had to kneel and do the deed. He smelt horrible, there seemed to be rolls of fat everywhere, I was bent up but crouched down, a big roll of fat over my head, with this man in my mouth and him grunting and swearing whilst Jeff kept watch at the corner. It ended in the usual manner, his pal going off mumbling thanks to Jeff who came close to me and kissed me, full on. I thought I couldn't be shocked anymore, he had done loads more sexually explicit things to me by then, but none more intimate, and asked me if I had enjoyed it. What do you say to something like that? I just shrugged, resigned to my fate and as he pushed me to my knees again, he took his turn.

There weren't many times like that. I think I worried him a little, as afterwards I had said I was going home and obviously upset. When I got home, I wanted to rush in and tell my parents what had happened, but they looked so content sitting there in the lounge watching TV. I knew if I did there would be an uproar, and I wasn't sure I would be believed anyway, as after 'the shed', I had been looked upon as sexually provocative and trouble. I let it go. They said something like, 'Oh didn't know you were home this week-end?' and carried on as normal. How could things be any worse anyway?

I would, before moving on, like to portray one other feeling. The abuse lasted six years, during which time I was growing, developing etc. I should have had 'normal' experiences, had contact with girls, done all the things a pre- and post-pubescent young male should have done. I learned to shave, I grew hair in all the right places, my voice lowered, I developed my body along fairly normal lines and was, I was told, quite good-looking, but underneath that almost every night I was degraded, used. My young, growing body, typical for a teenager, was being used, abused, dirtied; I lost all respect for myself, not once but many times.

50

Many, many times I would spend the night half-choking whilst he fucked my mouth. The usual scenario was him lying on his back with hips slightly swivelled, his right leg over my upper body holding it in place as he thrust into me, my head under the duvet, close to his groin, sweat, smells of sex, pubic hair in my face, in my nostrils until he grunted out his lust and then, even worse, him going into that hazy after-sex lull, me still pinioned beneath him, unable to move, his penis now soft but still quite large in my mouth, sticky, smelly.

Sometimes he would fall asleep, to my relief, and I would spend the whole night fighting for breath in the same position, under the duvet, him in my mouth (he rarely let me go from this spider-like embrace). After a short while I would feel him growing in my mouth again, moving slightly to enhance the feeling, and knowing 'Oh God' it was going to happen again. The smell of sex and sperm, I don't think I will ever forget that smell. Like death only living, yes, a living death, one from which there seemed no escape.

It went on and on and on. Sometimes being 'lent' to a mate for some favour or other; once in a public loo he had got frisky, started on me, taken me into a cubicle, and someone had been looking through a hole in the wall. Jeff had noticed and made me put on a bit of a show for the watcher, who put his own penis through the hole. You can guess what I had to do next. It didn't matter by then, I was too far gone for it to worry me, don't feel don't hurt.

In the later years I realised he had been fucking Sarah all the time too, but not letting me near her, we were his two little pets satisfying his separate needs. Once I was allowed to have her, which is when I found out he WAS having her, on the steps of some flats they were building by his house. I had gone to find him as dinner was nearly ready, and came across them after hearing all-too-familiar noises from them, he was fucking her, she spread out on an old carpet, naked. He stopped when I appeared, got off and lay beside her and motioned me to have a go. God forgive me, but I did. I had wanted a woman SO badly after the shed incident, the thought of that night had never left me, the thought that she too was suffering what I was at his hands never entered my brain until much later in life when, in talking to her, we shared so many

51

similar feelings and thoughts, and to this day we almost shun each other if we pass in life, I think because of what seeing each other brings back. But on that day, I had her, boy did I have her, entering her for the second time in my life, but this time with a body almost full grown and a manhood to match and after, as she lay there with a blank look in her eyes, my ejaculation leaking from her inner thigh, her soft lower lips pink and pouting from my ministrations, he knelt and licked her, then had her himself as I watched. Just before he finished he reached down, grabbed my manhood, pulled on it roughly, seeming to find pleasure in hurting not only her with his hard, rough strokes, but me also with his squeezing. He came finally, almost bashing her with himself. I saw her wince as he groaned, but not so he could see.

Sarah, if you ever read this, forgive me.

So it continued for six years until I left school. I had no further reason to stay at nan's. I don't think she ever knew what went on, who knows? By then, though, the damage was done. I was a survivor, I had carried on living, and that is all the good that can be said about my life until then: I was still alive.

I followed the path life led me on. I had no real skills. I knew how to 'read' people perhaps, and had a certain insight into people and their problems, learnt from many, many years of 'sussing out' people to give them their needs so they would like me. Maybe a little of mum's 'power' was in me, who knows.

I never had a girlfriend; come to think of it, I never had male friends either. I certainly wasn't interested in 'boyfriends', male sex was part of my life for the reasons I have given and, in truth, vented my sexual tension somewhat, but to instigate a relationship with another male never entered my head. I wanted girls, but who would want me, soiled as I was?

I was on the whole pretty mixed up, every time I had an erection or felt sexually aroused seemed to be around the things going on with Jeff. I questioned myself as to my sexuality. Was I gay? Bi? Straight? Well, I couldn't be straight, could I? I got aroused, I let another male do the things he did, I did (albeit forcibly) sexual things to another male, what did that make me? I came off with another man, surely that meant I must be wrong. I knew I felt horrible, guilty, but underneath it all I wanted a girl. The feeling of entering a woman, fucking her, being part of her, joined, it was brilliant. I wanted THAT. Not what I did, and each time it happened with Jeff, I felt even dirtier.

But how do you make something like that go away? You can't change the past. I had done it, his stuff was inside me, continued to be inside me, it was no use stopping. I was past redemption – I felt it was too late.

I left school with no qualifications, my teachers tutting and shaking their heads and saying stuff like, 'You have a brain in your head, why don't you use it, boy?' I never worked for a year after leaving school. Despite not being wanted at home, I retired to my bedroom and became almost a hermit, no, I WAS a hermit. I never went out, never did anything, and my memories of that year are of sleeping almost constantly. It was only as the result of another incident that I broke this spell.

I did not see anything of Jeff after leaving school. I didn't want that any more – truth be told, I never wanted it, but it had happened and that was that.

It's funny how my life seems to be affected by things happening in twos, as again two things happened to change my life. One, my great-nan died and I had occasion to be at nan's again as she had to go to the funeral across country, and I was asked to stay with Jeff for company. I knew the real reason and tried to argue against it, but unsuccessfully. My parents thought it would 'do me good' to get out for a few days. I stayed the weekend with him, what hell! From Friday around 5 p.m. to Monday morning at 9 a.m., it was utter hell. Constant sex, constant degradation. I had been a year on my own, had tried to forget what had happened, but this person had such power over me. I just can't explain, he whined, cajoled, threatened, bullied, took me so many times I felt sick. Had me doing things so degrading I felt less than dirt – and I did them. To this day I ask myself why? Why did I let it happen? But I did.

The worst bit was on Sunday evening, after having almost exhausted himself sexually on me, he invented this 'game' which in itself doesn't sound too bad; it involved a bottle of ink and a piece of electrical wire. We had been acting out 'doctors and patients', a classic with him, he got to examine you and do whatever he wanted in the process, giving you all sorts of sexual

53

'medicine' to make you supposedly better. Then it was his turn. He was quite sated, having just relieved his sexual tension in an hour-long 'examination' of my body, and relevant treatment, so was lying across a lounge chair (we had the house to ourselves and had not worn clothes since Friday night). He made me examine him, paying attention to me treating him by oral cleaning of his genitals, then he dipped one end of the wire into the bottle of ink and gave me the wire, saying, 'If you put the clean end of the wire into the end of my knob, it means you are mine forever to do as I want with. If you put the end with the ink on it in, I will die a slow painful death.' This was pretty normal stuff from him: mental blackmail was a daily thing, he had a way of making you believe anything he said.

He then pretended to go to sleep, saying I had five minutes to 'treat him'. God, my brain whizzed. I was battered, used, tired and had just endured 48 hours of endless, relentless abuse. My body ached, my brain swam and I felt as if my world was somewhere else, not part of this world. I took the wire, the answer to my problems (just wire and plain ink, for God's sake, but you had to be there) and dipped the ink-filled end into the end of his penis.

A wave of relief shot through me, for an instant I was free of it all, then he moved, looked, looked at me and groaned. Oh God, did he groan. John Gielgud move over, as for the rest of that night he gave the best performance of dying I ever saw. I was mortified. In my semi-madness I thought I was really killing him, that I had done the unthinkable, it was all my fault. I slept not a wink that night, he made me suck it the whole night long to 'remove the poison', he said, his only hope of living. He writhed, he groaned, he cramped and feigned unconsciousness.

I was in such a state of panic. I would be arrested, thrown into a gaol, punished beyond bearability. All through the night he acted, all through the night I grovelled, like a whipped dog, a mongrel at his heel. Yet again I thought nothing could get worse, this was worse, much worse. At 9 a.m. my nan came back, we were still naked, still in the lounge, still in the throes of feigned death. I was almost insane with panic, my hair stood on end, my brain ached, oh how it ached. I was in agony of guilt and fear, and as the door went with my nan returning home, he jumped so quickly I thought it was all over and I would have to explain to my nan how I had killed Jeff, but instead he ran upstairs, seemingly fit and well, leaving me there, naked and near hysteria, to explain myself.

He appeared two minutes or so later, dressed, looking perfectly okay, and looked at me as if to say 'What's the matter with you?' I had a feeling after that day my nan was not so naïve after all: she found me naked in that much of a state I could hardly talk, shaking like a leaf, but never questioned what had gone on. That was the power my Uncle Jeff had.

The other thing was an hour or so after. I was so upset I made to leave. Jeff said he would walk with me a short way, as he had to phone about a job interview (and incidentally on the way try to persuade me never to reveal what had happened that weekend, he knew he had frightened me badly). I, too, was out of work. When we got to the phone box, after he had worked his evil magic on me, I had agreed to keep quiet in exchange for having a chance at the job interview. So instead of him phoning for it, I did. They said come straight down, I did (anything to get away from Jeff) and I still don't know how, considering the state I was in, but I got the job, to start the very next day. I was now a hospital porter.

I was just 18.

And I was never with Jeff again.

LISA

I loved my job. It may sound kind of menial to some, but to me it was manna from heaven. I worked, lived and spent most of my waking time in an environment of a caring, ordered establishment. It was the main hospital for my home city, so was quite large, I worked shifts and found the reason I had got the job so easily was that they had trouble finding people to tolerate the long hours involved. Well, it fitted my needs fine. I was still living at home at this time, but the longer I spent away from it the better as far as I was concerned.

The BIGGEST bonus to me, though, had to be THE NURSES. Let me explain: you know my background up to now, I hope I have given some flavour of how it was. I had learned to 'put on the mask' to deal with life, outwardly. People didn't see me, they saw the person I thought they wanted to see, bubbly, bright, not a care in the world, happy-go-lucky (I know now there must be a lot of people reading this who identify with that, but then I thought I was the only one living a 'false' life). I was very popular: people came to me to tell me their troubles, share their burdens, I had the knack of knowing just what to say and the right body language and intonation to make them feel better. I was (and still am really) a caring, sharing person. I used to sit sometimes, when I had a quiet moment, which wasn't very often as I filled my life up with 'stuff', and think, I wonder what people would think if they saw the real me? But they never did, as if I had shown them I just KNOW they would have shunned and hated me for what I had done. So I became this 'person', Mr Fantastic; all my energy and time was spent on being Mr Personality. I cared, I nurtured, I took time for people, I made people laugh, feel good for a moment or two which, in a hospital environment, went down a storm.

Patients loved me, my boss thought I was brilliant, I had for the first time 'mates', within the porter staff, we used to go out drinking together. I finally felt I was moving towards my life aims, to be 'normal'.

Inside, well, that was a different thing, but I was young, and when you're young you bend and stretch easily into life's twists and turns. I knew, I just knew I wouldn't ever be with a woman on a proper footing; no one was going to want me. I was sure that despite all my best efforts, women could see through me like a piece of glass, see my wickedness, see me with Jeff and the things that had happened, and although I was extremely popular it was, I felt, in a sisterly way as far as women were concerned. I figured my only sex appeal must be to other men as that is what had happened with Jeff, so I must be unconsciously giving out signals in the wrong language, and women, being far superior to me, must know that. I spent lots of brainpower making sure my male colleagues didn't get the wrong ones now. The last thing I wanted was more of that, but my body ached for female company and I was surrounded by it daily. It was fantastic and also a little sad, ha, ha, it felt a bit like a starving man in a cake shop but with no teeth to eat with, ha, ha.

I soon learned to obtain dentures!

I had been there for about six months, pretty uneventfully, just settling in and getting to know people, finding my way round. My social life was pretty good, there were lots of parties, plenty going on, and with my personality I fitted right in with it all. I bought new clothes, felt motivated for the first time in ages and started to take some pride in my appearance and style. I felt good.

I often observe young people nowadays; I have become a bit of a psychological watcher. As I have learned more about myself through life, I have realised my life had NOT been normal up until then, as I had thought, and it has led me to look at others to see what their lives are all about. You know, if you look at youngsters, I don't think they have changed much in general from when I was younger, despite modern technology rearing its head. If you look, there still is that transition people go through from one stage of their lives to the next, like small gates or hurdles being finally jumped, and then galloping on to the next one. I was stuck behind one such hurdle, the inability, or seeming inability to attract the opposite sex, and I'm pretty sure if you spoke to ten teenage boys today, six would say the same.

My hurdle was jumped one night at a party in the doctors' quarters. There was the normal dancing, drinking, flirting etc., and one of the doctors, who was quite young, commented on my being so popular 'with the ladies', and how he wished he could be so successful. Well, that gave me a new slant on things. Obviously others saw things differently to me.

The same night, a girl called Swizz (nickname) who I fancied tremendously, and who not only had a bit of a reputation, but seemed to be in high demand amongst the male staff of the hospital, got quite drunk and made a pass at me. I was delighted. There, in front of the whole crowd, she had picked ME out to be her consort for the evening. I had pulled after all, wheheyyy!! (I put aside the fact she was drunk, had just had a row with her latest boyfriend and was probably trying to make him jealous. I just knew a good thing when it felt me – literally, I mean, she was quite drunk.)

We spent the night together. Boy, I nearly floated out of her room the next morning. I swear my feet didn't touch the ground; I was on a high so high I felt like I was flying. I thought, 'Hey, people don't know and if I don't tell them, they will NEVER know.' The mask person was a success. All I had to do was keep being the mask, simple, bloody simple. Why hadn't I thought of it before? Life was easy.

My sex life took off like Concorde. I got laid by half the nursing staff, was the envy of all my pals and dodged between partying, shagging and keeping my job, as it was slightly frowned upon. A lowly porter going with nurses, they were a cut above us according to management, so whilst I knew they frowned on my activities I was extra-specially good at my job to keep people happy, and juggled my private life to fit around supposed decency rules. Being a porter, though, had its advantages; I had keys in the porter's room for the whole hospital. I knew every door and window in the nurses' home, I could come and go almost any hour

le (Nanin) aged 8 or 9, abuse at its worst

Dad, Mum and me, 'happy family' photo taken by Uncle Jeff

ay after 'Rugby Pub' incident, Dad taking proof he bought me drink following g row (feel the tension)

My four beautiful sons (who could ask for anything more)

Boys and me, growing up in 'happy times'

Balcony in Rhodes on my birthday

Beach in Australia where 'Nanin' lies at rest

Self portrait of author, 4.30 a.m., day after coming out of hospital, and typing last chapter all night to finish book (rough, but relieved!)

unnoticed, apart from whoever was on duty at night, and even then usually got an envious look like, 'You lucky sod' when I was seen leaving a room at 4 a.m. or something. I was happy, having a whale of a time and felt good in myself.

I was seeing a Casualty nurse when I first saw Lisa. I had learned there were rules amongst the ladies when dating: you did not 'butterfly' if you wanted a serious relationship. It was okay to go out with different people if you did it over short spells, a couple of weeks each, because they knew you were not serious and therefore no one got hurt. 'Butterflying' meant many partners in one week, you were then a tart, and only got laid afterwards by dogs (those young ladies who did it with anyone, anytime, anywhere, sometimes called 'martinis').

If you wanted a decent person, you followed the rules. Maggie, my current, in Casualty, was such a person. I had been dating her for about a month, sex was very good, usually in the car or up an entry on the way back from the pub, taking her back to mine was like the kiss of death, and her parents would have castrated me if they had know half we got up to, but I liked the situation anyway, it was free and easy, spontaneous.

I almost killed us once though when we decided on a long session in the car and, after driving about for a while and not finding anywhere suitable, and it being late January and pretty cold, parked in the garage where I kept the car and got down to it with the engine running and the door shut for privacy, and woke later (post-coital nap) to exhaust fumes everywhere and barely able to breathe. We laughed about it afterwards, but it was a pretty stupid thing to do at the time.

Anyway things were going fine with Maggie, when I walked past the nurses' training unit one day and a fresh group of trainee nurses came out and nearly bumped into me. (Nurses spent the first three months in training 'block', so weren't seen for a while before being let loose on the wards.) I made light of it, cracked a joke or something, got a few laughs, but in amongst the young women there one stuck out, she was beautiful. I mean really stunningly beautiful, tall slender neck – that neck still haunts me today, it was the kind of neck you wanted to snuggle into, to kiss and run your lips up against, like a swan. She had a lovely oval face, deep brown eyes that took you in and drowned you, a slim size 10 body, with breasts just the right size, you know, absolutely the right proportion to the rest of her body, and such a sweet 'little miss innocent' smile. She took my breath away; it was lust at first sight. I didn't know it but I had met Lisa, my future wife.

I didn't think I had a hope in hell of going out with her, as although there was only a year or so between our ages, she was such a sweet, young, pretty, innocent thing and I was such a beat-up, been around, 'Sid James' type. I figured she would never go for me. The nurses I had gone for up until then had all been nice, pretty and perfectly acceptable, but Lisa was special, she was a cut about the ordinary, she was truly stunningly beautiful.

I wooed and courted her anyway; I used every trick in the book I had learned. I still kept Maggie going, just in case, and that was nearly my downfall. I was 'butterflying'. I figured I had little chance with Lisa, a steady thing with Maggie, so I should hedge my bets – wrong. Funnily enough, though, it was them finding out about each other that finally got me a date with Lisa.

You can't keep anything a secret for long in a close community like that: nurses talked, gossiped, who fancied who, who had said what, when and to whom. Apparently there had nearly been a fight in the canteen when Maggie had overhead Lisa saying something about this porter fancying her. As they were on adjoining tables it all came out. Maggie got mad as hell with me (as she should), and finished our relationship, telling all and sundry of the other nurses what a bastard I was, and I thought that was that with me. No more nurses. I had seen it before when someone had broken the unwritten rule, they were 'out' as far as dating went. It had done my reputation the world of good with the other lads, funnily enough, they looked at me with a look that said, 'How the hell does an ugly old bastard like that do it?' and 'Wish it was ME in that position'. But amongst the nurses I was dead dog meat. I had done the dirty on one of them, and although I knew I was now thought of as a 'ladies' man (life-long ambition), I knew with the rest of the nursing staff I wouldn't get anywhere with them until I had 'proved' I could be a little more ethical in my relationships. I settled to a bout of celibacy.

Strangely enough, though, I bumped into Lisa one day in

Outpatients. We were both off duty and heading for the canteen, and she asked me why I had done it, been with Maggie, and tried it on with her. Don't ask me why but I told her the truth, that I figured I hadn't a hope with her but had tried anyway as I thought she was something very special. Well, blow me down she said she thought I was very special too, she had heard of my reputation amongst the other nurses, had in fact been warned against any contact with me, but found the fact I was a bit of a ladies' man attractive and yes, she would LOVE to go out with me on condition we did it properly. Thank you God! Oh thank, you, thank you.

Should I say here, yes I think so, Lisa, if you ever read this (and I have obviously changed people's names to protect them, but you know who you are), Lisa, I am so, so sorry. I look back on that day and almost wish you had told me to get lost. I did it, didn't I? I took something special and wrecked it. I am so, so sorry.

We dated, I loved it, I used to walk down the road with Lisa on my arm and feel a million dollars. She was (probably still is) stunning, a real beauty. I nearly had a fight once when we passed this good-looking guy when out one night and he stopped Lisa and said something quietly in her ear. When I asked what, she told me he had said what was she doing with an ugly old tosser like me when she could have been with him. Well, I flew back up the street incensed and made him apologise to me and her. Looking back, he was big enough to have flattened me, but anger is a powerful thing and I think he sensed my anger well.

I think that started the downward trail even then. We had only been going out a few months, but even then my insecurity showed through the cracks in my mask, because that was who Lisa was going out with – the mask, not me.

Conversely enough, I feel if I had shown her the real me then we would probably still be together now. She went for honesty and I was living a lie, my whole life was a lie.

I didn't though, and trouble started, her parents never approved of me. Sixth sense? Who knows? When I visited her house I was met with courteous disdain, they imposed all kinds of restrictions on her, home by 10 p.m., having to tell them whenever she was meeting me and where we were going. She ended up leaving home because of me as, after a huge row one night over the restrictions they were putting on her, she ran out in tears and I met her on the corner of the street (I was on my way up to see her), with her mum shouting at her, and when Lisa got in my car she was given the ultimatum by her mum that if she went with me that night, she needn't come home again. Lisa came to live at my parents actually, which put more strain on my relationship with them. They loved Lisa, thought she was lovely, I think they had the feeling she was much too good for me, but they let her share a bedroom with Dee, my young sister, who was by now 12 or 13.

Things came to a head at home a few months later, when the hospital authorities, getting to know Lisa was living with me (albeit in separate rooms), sacked her for gross misconduct (fraternisation with other staff). By this time I had been warned myself for the same thing (I think Maggie had confirmed what they had suspected) and I too was sacked from my job.

I had lost Lisa her career, her family, her friends and the future she had planned for herself. I made a resolve that day to pay her back with lifelong 'making good'. I had a stunning beauty as a partner, people envied me, I would prove myself to Lisa, she had faith in me, had stuck by me and we were best friends.

They say life is a winding road. I think it made us even stronger in our resolve to 'beat the system'. If things hadn't gone the way they had, would we have stayed together so long? Who knows? I do know that we both would show the world we were right and they were wrong: two months later, we married.

Looking back, as hindsight so often shows, it wasn't much of a basis to start a marriage with, was it? Two people in the shite together, and the way out we chose? To spend the rest of our lives together...

I was so desperate to 'belong' to someone, she I think desperate to 'show' people. I had a beautiful wife; she had a lifelong debt being repaid. I suppose it was okay for a bit, we both got out of it what we needed at the time, but as the basis for a lifelong commitment, I'm not sure about that.

We bought a small two-up, two-down house (we both quickly found other work, me as a driver, Lisa as a hairdresser), and tried to settle down to married life. Again, looking back, we were a couple of naïve, stupid kids, fresh out in life and still wet behind the ears, but we tried.

Our house, although cheaply furnished, was ours, we had independence from others, a new-found freedom we both loved, and were able to try out new ways of life and living that weren't hampered by grown-ups per se. This was the swinging seventies, forget the sixties, they were just testing the water for our generation, we felt. Life was wide open, our social life was still pretty good, there was this whole ideology of freedom around, you could do anything if you so wanted, nothing was unobtainable.

We had people back to stay at ours, other couples became our friends, we started to join the 'in' crowd, ha, ha. It sounds so dated now, but at the time we thought we were IT.

I can't put a finger on just when it started: too many parties, too much booze, the wrong company? But my innocent little virgin and I became part of the culture. To me, I had nothing to lose in joining this swinging culture, sex was freedom, free love man, and all that. I had hair down to my waist, flared jeans and flower power shirts. Lisa wore micro minis, hot pants (remember them?) and kinky boots up to her armpits. It was 'normal', or so we thought.

I do remember, however, the first time I realised Lisa had slept with someone else, a gut-wrenching feeling. Outwardly I hardly flinched, accepted, as I had done so many times before, a situation I did not like but had no power over. I made no rules for Lisa to follow; we were free spirits, together through mutual consent (deep down I couldn't believe my luck that this beauty wanted to be with me, so to keep her I let her have full rein). So how could I deal with this sanely and rationally? There I was with my past, a dark secret past (Jeff, the abuse, my dad); an open, well-known past at the hospital, and a world I lived in that congratulated people who threw off the confines of the 'dark ages' of conformity and who were liberated, free, a person who had absolutely no moral standards whatsoever, whose body was an open book read by many, and married to this stunning beauty who I should encourage to be liberated and free, and balanced against that, the feeling deep down that I had finally found someone special, clean and fresh, who wanted ME. That was the important bit, someone who had all those qualities and had still chosen ME, who now took

63

away that specialness and became like everyone else I knew, free and easy. I just could not come to terms with it. I dealt with it like I had dealt with everything else in my life: my famous saying, 'If you don't feel, it can't hurt you'. I buried it all deep down with the rest and got on with life.

Time passed: I think I lost respect for Lisa from then. It sounds silly I know, but I felt I had nothing to lose, but she was very special in that she was still clean, and knowing she was doing what she did made her as bad as me. Conversely, how the hell did she KNOW I was not like her – all I showed her was the mask, so from her point of view we were equal. God, what a mess I was!

Four sons came along. I am not particularly religious – I always had the feeling I had been somewhat abandoned in that direction at that time, but God, thank you for my sons. I had something finally I could believe in, they became my life work. I wanted to give them everything, to guide their lives through childhood and see them protected and safe, SAFE into their adulthood. They would have what I had not, love, safety and a secure upbringing.

Time went on. I made sure we had a secure home, I built a surroundings around them I knew they would feel loved and secure in, we moved once then stayed the next 18 years in the same house. The boys grew, life went on, and if one day I get to the pearly gates (if they exist) and old Pete asks me for a memory of life I will tell him of Christmases with my boys and Lisa. Wonderful, wonderful times, those times could not, with all the wizardry in Hollywood, be recreated by Walt Disney even, log fire, Christmas lights, carol singing, Yuletide Christmases straight out of mythology and brought to real life for my children. To see their faces, to live for those days, made every single trial and tribulation I have ever gone through worth every pain. I would go through slow painful deaths ten times to recreate those Christmases again just once.

I am crap at loads of stuff; I have been known to be a real bastard sometimes. I have 'cocked up' big-time on more than one occasion, but at those Christmases I excelled. I have a gift, perhaps self-taught I don't know, but I can make a home. I can turn an empty room into somewhere you want to stay, that you feel comfortable and relaxed in. I have an artistic flair I am sometimes ashamed of, in case it makes me less than masculine – that doubt from my past experiences haunts me to this day – but at home-making I am good.

We were together 21 years, Lisa and I – didn't do too bad, did we? The last four or five years were hell, but before that we managed, grew I think into comfortable acceptance. I don't think I ever fell in love with Lisa, nor she with me, but we loved each other in a fashion – companionship, friendship and perhaps a need to be wanted by someone. Is that enough for a lifelong marriage? I don't know. It was enough for a long time anyway.

So the boys were happy, growing up nicely. I was content? I suppose so. I had a family around me, a woman who wanted to be with me, a nice home, car, caravan, holidays, all the trappings of success, or so I thought. Lisa? I guess she was reasonably happy, I felt often a rumble, a feeling of unease with her, that things were not right in her deepest feelings, but I thought that was just minor things and that overall she was okay.

I learned at a much later date that she thought me overbearing, in control of everything, and a 'power mad' husband. Was I? Maybe I was. To me, I simply took the reins of leadership in our relationship. I organised things, made sure everything was going the way I thought was right, I never felt I 'fettered' her; if she wanted to do something, I encouraged, helped, did all I could to fulfil her wishes, or so I thought. She would say (has said) that everything had to go through me; perhaps she was right. I only know my intentions were honourable and I wanted to do my best for my family in making their lives as happy as possible, but I suppose in striving so hard to make things work and to get things right, I perhaps did have too much say in everything.

Our sex life was open as our marriage was: I had affairs, she had affairs, all with the consent of the other. The rules, albeit unspoken, were that the other knew about it and there were no secrets anywhere. I felt if I knew, I could deal with it. And again that feeling, that how do you stop a rolling stone, it had happened that was our life, stopping now could not make it whole again. The tear was there, ragged and flapping, best make a feature of it as there was no way to invisibly mend it.

Since early on I think we had lost respect for each other, we had become commodities, horrible I know, but that's how it was. So we played about. I tried not to think about things too deeply; I felt being 'the stud' with other women was what made a man, forever then fighting the legacy of Jeff. I became good at what I did, I could 'satisfy' women totally, and something else: I was wanted by someone, needed by them, it boosted my ego, which was pretty low anyway.

With Lisa, strange, and also feeding my neurosis, when she came back from 'being out' and got into bed with me, I knew what she had done, knew I had been cuckolded, but the knowledge somehow fed my need to be punished. I was dirty from before, so if the cleanest, nicest thing in my life was dirty now too, I felt almost on the same level, as if it was somehow okay. And making love at those times (I always did to 'reclaim' her) was the most satisfying sex ever. Also I still had visions for the sake of masturbation of 'the shed' day, all tied in together, I became not only accustomed to, but actively encouraging of, her being freshly taken by someone.

It almost makes me sick now to think that all that happened, but on top of my younger years' experiences it didn't seem too bad, a lesser evil if you like. God, I was a mess!

Time went on, life went on. I survived. I made the best of what life dealt me but never actively sought to change things. I was, in my head, lucky to have what I had. The spare room in my head where I locked all the monsters became fuller and fuller and fuller.

One day the walls caved in and all the monsters and demons came rushing out into my life and overpowered me.

THE BOUGH BREAKS

Of all the words I have so far written, the next few are the hardest for me. What was my living nightmare woke up and became my daily hell.

I don't even try to put down the feelings behind these words, not consciously anyway; you are, I'm sure, intelligent enough to do that yourselves. I have spoken to many people in my life, some of whom have said, compared to the holocaust your problems are insignificant; alongside the terminally-ill child in hospital, it is small fry. I agree. I also thank whoever it is up there or out there for sparing me those things.

I also know those things didn't happen to me, but what did happen to me, HAPPENED TO ME ...

When you hear of a plane crash or a serious illness befalling a friend it is bad: you 'feel' for that person, have sympathy for them, it is a horrible thing to happen. Then after a few weeks or months, sad to say, you accept it. It is old news, it happened to someone else out there, removed and bad as it is, your life goes on untouched for the main part.

When it happens to you, it is a whole new ball of string. This is personal, it affects YOU, and your life is changed irrevocably forever. If your friend's mum dies, that's bad, if YOUR mum dies, that's devastating. These things had not happened to my friend, they had happened to me. It was personal, and no matter how thankful I am for a greater ill not befalling me, the ills that did befall me were real and in MY life.

Why do I write? I don't really know. To 'let it out', to justify or help justify my life and the things I have done? I suppose all of those, but I think mainly to say sorry, I am genuinely sorry. I have

67

fucked up a lot of lives in my own living, my ills have spilled over and affected others, and for that I am truly sorry. I think this next bit tells how I fucked up most and to them I want to say, sorry.

There is a nursery rhyme that comes into my head thinking of this next bit: 'When the bough breaks, the baby will fall'. My bough broke, and the little boy called Nanin in me fell a very long way and woke up.

Things were getting worse day by day. It seemed that my life was going nowhere, I listened to others, heard of the male menopause, mid-life crisis; I was 39½, was that it? I felt 'full' of everything, but that my whole existence was for nothing, where was I in all this, who was I? And again, two things happened.

Within 18 months of each other my parents died. About two months after, I heard Jeff had died. All the monsters in my head burst open and it all spilled out into my life. I became mentally unhinged; I couldn't see it from my side of my eyeballs, but I was. The two people who had imposed all those confines and hurt in my life, my dad and Jeff, were gone. I no longer had to fear them, they could not get me anymore, their power was broken. I was free.

I suddenly felt all-powerful, all-knowing, the dam had broken, all this 'stuff' was coming out. I still didn't let it out, not from my head anyway, it just had no room to contain it any more and flooded around my head, my thoughts and my life like a storm at sea. I used to describe my feelings afterwards as doggy-paddling in deep water, looking for something solid to hold onto. I was drowning and I didn't know how to swim, didn't know how to breathe hardly in this liquid hell inside my head.

I started doing strange things. I searched for some kind of solidity and, having found none in my life, imposed solidity in those around me – namely my family, nothing moved unless it went through me. I had total power as I've said. I had always I suppose 'supervised' things, but now I controlled everything, down to the last detail. My past sexuality hit me in the face like a brick; memories came flooding back like tidal waves. The mask was holding on by just a few flakes of skin, what was behind battered my thoughts to be let out. What the hell was happening to me?

I wanted to sort things out. I had lost 39 years of life somewhere, been existing, just running on tickover all that time, whilst the mask, what other people wanted, ran my very being. I was nothing, now I was something, wasn't I? My head hummed, my brain hurt, I struggled each and every second to come to terms with these feelings. All that hurt, all that damage, all that degradation. I had killed my unborn twin, I had become a sex freak, homosexual, dominated by a paedophilic uncle, I had been a failure to my parents. I couldn't even die and give them what they wanted, a girl. I had open sex with other women. I allowed my wife to have sex with other men – not only that, I enjoyed it. Did I? I must have, at least, I let it happen. I was not a man, I was not a person, I was a monster. How could I live with myself? I decided in the fog of my insanity to regain me, to try everything I could, to go on a spree of self-indulgence that rivalled a starving man feasting on a banquet. I had no justification for all this except an overwhelming feeling of being cheated somehow, I have been cheated of my life, and now by God, I was going to make up for it. I had been hurt, oh so hurt, I would let all that hurt out. How? I didn't know, yes I did, if I had been hurt then I would hurt everybody else.

What the hell was I thinking? But I wasn't, was I? Thinking. I couldn't think straight; I was just drowning in all this stuff. My poor family, oh how sorry I am now, too late maybe. I ruled with an iron rod, my kids jumped when I barked, I was in control. My wife slept with others and I got a kick out of it, right, I would organise her sleeping with others. Not only that, I would show her some of my past, I would join in and show her the REAL me, the dirty, sordid me. I would show her so much pain in me by re-enacting my past experiences whilst in her company, she would fall to my side, take me in her arms and say how sorry she was, how much she loved me and would help me, she would rescue me. Yes, she would rescue me, I would be saved and I would no longer have to be the mask. She would see the real me, no not the real me, oh dear this was all so confusing. I would show her me being degraded, show her a glimpse of what I had suffered, what I had done, and she would understand, forgive me, absolve me even.

My brain reeled, a giddy whirl of hurt, anger, frustration. I thought, 'I'll show her, I'll show them all.' How the hell I

69

expected poor Lisa to understand I do not know. I was not sane then, I was mad. Yes, I was mad, right round the twist.

There followed a year, two maybe, of living, waking, worse nightmare hell. I watched my boys fall apart, I watched them start to hate me, horror took me at what was happening. I organised group sex sessions with my wife and joined in myself, anything went. I was dirty, disgusting, the lowest of the low, so if I did this I was being 'normal'. It was right (God knows where my logic came from), and it served her right if she got hurt, why didn't she understand? I felt the hurt I was experiencing shone out from behind my eyes like a torch, but she could not see it. I loved her, but I also hated her for not saving me. No one had ever saved me, not my parents, not Lisa, no one. Fuck them all then. I would show them hurt. I would hurt them so much they would know what it was like, how I felt for a change, and my dream or my nightmare continued. Maybe, just maybe they might understand and save me now.

Guess what? I came home from work one day just after Christmas, and they had gone. All of them. It had worked; I had hurt them so much they had broken too.

I ask for no sympathy. I deserved everything I got, but I ask you to know that whilst I sit here now writing this, I can hardly see the page for the tears that flow from me.

I am sorry Lisa, I am so, so sorry boys. I know you will never forgive me. I can only say I am so, so sorry.

My neighbour just knocked at my door to see if I was all right as she could hear crying. I hope God hears my crying and hears my prayers for forgiveness. What I put them through. God help me, and please God, help them.

This was the worst point I think in my entire life. I had not had much control over what had happened earlier. Nanin was a little boy. I was, however, responsible for what had happened now, I, I had done it, I could not pass on the blame, could not justify my actions. The only thing I had ever been good at and the only clean things that had ever been in my life, my home and my boys, and I had frightened as much as I had been frightened. I was the monster now, all kinds of worms opened up with this thought. Was there the same justification for Jeff's actions? Did his father hold the responsibility for his abusive behaviour? Memory came back of something I had heard as a child whilst hiding in my fridge space, that my eldest brother was not my father's, that my granddad had something, mysteriously, to do with it. Was that why my dad was like he was, wanting justification for his own hang-ups? God, oh God, oh God . . .

I ran every combination and scenario in the book through my head, trying to find a solution, and none came. The times I had caught a look or an action, however small, that just did not 'feel' right – the way my granddad used to carry round Jeff all the time. When you're young you know no better, but instinct still warns you of possible danger, like an inbuilt radar, and I, in my tenuous position within the family unit, had felt that feeling often. I took stock of my family, my dad, mum, Jeff, my granddad, my nan staying with dad overnight, my brothers and Sarah, what was I looking at? What was fact and what was fiction? I lived in a council area where sex was rife amongst everyone, young and old: my whole world, upbringing, life's experiences were all of the same ilk, what the hell was going on? And I felt myself slip even further down the ladder to despair.

The divorce was a messy one, no access to the boys, no contact with Lisa, lots of debt, loss of my job, it went on and on. I decided on a surefire way to cure things.

I would die.

God would forgive me if I died, I would pay the final payment for stealing my twin's life, I would give up my own. Lisa and the boys would have a fresh start, they would be glad I was dead I was sure, and selfishly, I suppose, I would no longer be living this nightmare. Yes, I would die.

You can count on the fingers of one hand true friends. Thankfully, two of mine lived across the road.

I had known Jack and Jane for 15 years (funny how my life seemed to be influenced by the initial 'J'). They were, and still are, the happily married family unit I so longed to be. They had seen Lisa go that day and hovered in the background, giving support to me throughout the whole time. On the day I decided to end it all, luckily Jack was sitting in his lounge, which faced over my front garden, and in his words 'watched a usually knackered and gaunt-looking me come out of my house and saunter off as if I hadn't a care in the world'. Alarm bells rang, and when I came back a little later carrying a chemist's bag they really started to worry. (I had had to buy a few other things in the chemist's along with the paracetamol to avoid suspicion.) Clear thinking, forward planning, ha, a touch of saneness in all this insanity, I finally had the perfect answer . . . or so I thought.

I went in home, took all the tablets, put the fire on (didn't want to be cold), lay down on the settee and waited for death. Job done.

I never heard the phone ringing. Jack and Jane had left it half an hour, pondering between being intrusive and being caring, and had tried to ring me. He tells me by this time the hairs on the back of his neck were standing on end as he just KNEW something wasn't right.

They decided to come over and check. They had a spare key for my place as they used to feed the cat whilst we were away on holiday, and thankfully they found me in time. Ambulances, hospitals, stomach pumps, needles, oxygen, monitors, I vaguely remember them. The next week feeling like death warmed up, as indeed I was, and the start of many, many visits from shrinks, psychologists and 'mental health' units, (what a lovely name for it) that were to follow.

Jack, Jane, I owe you big-time. Thanks.

No, it wasn't over like that. I tried three more times, once with a rope and a tree and was discovered and had another stay 'inside', and again, the final time, when after parking my car in the drive at the rear of my house and connecting the hosepipe, starting the car and settling down for death, it ran out of petrol; and not being thwarted, moving into my house, half-dead, barricading the doors in the lounge with sheets etc. and putting on the gas fire without lighting it (no mean feat I can tell you with automatic ignition, but I did it) and again settling down to die, the gas went. I woke up around 3 a.m. having started the whole thing at about 10 p.m., feeling sick, freezing cold, totally exhausted and thinking 'This is obviously not meant to be'. I gave up trying to die from then on and let into my thoughts that maybe I would have to stay alive, and that if I had to do that I had better think of, or start to think of, ways that were less painful than these. I started concentrating on how to start living instead. All this had taken around a year; the divorce was through, Lisa had re-married (hope you're happy Lisa, truly I do). I had lost the marital home and moved into a flat, and was trying to decide where to go from there.

Don't get me wrong: it wasn't that clear-cut and easy; no contact with the boys almost destroyed me. I wrote a lot of poetry at this time (separate book), and in one of them the sentiment goes:

> I can feel the emptiness, since my partner left,
> Taking all our children, and leaving me bereft,
> I can see her laughter as she starts her life anew
> I wish her only happiness, but don't take my children too.

I missed them so much. My life became a constant round of doctors and hospitals, trying to face up to what had happened, to deal with reality and put some kind of straight line into the spaghetti that was me. I could not look at the real reason I felt this way, I know it sounds strange given what I have already written, but your mind just does not work in a straight line, it felt like six completely different music tracks and five TV stations all playing at full blast at the same time in your thoughts, and whilst you could tell Mantovani from Emmerdale you could not separate one from the other, they all ran into each other and you found yourself screaming from within, but no one could hear you, 'Turn the volume down'.

Before, if anyone had said the words 'mental health' I would have backed off a mile: 'nutters', 'insane', 'wierdos' are three of the words that spring to mind. Hide all the sharp objects and call an ambulance. In writing this I am seven years down the line, seven years ... I will come to that later, but those first few months, that first year or so, my goodness what an eye-opener!

Years ago they used to lock people up for simply having a baby whilst being unwed, or for being epileptic and so on. I think you would be driven to madness if put in a mental health unit sane; but broken as I was, it deadened the trauma. They kept me alive, they were there when everyone else wasn't, in the dead of night when the ghosts and ghoulies of your nightmares come to you and you could no longer fight them off, or the black, black cloud of

73

insanity, depression came over you, they were there with as much time, patience and skill as it needed to calm you and make you feel safe again. Some of my most vivid memories of being 'in' are of early hours of the morning, listening to the moans and shouts that are part of nightly routine in there, and being at an absolute and final low. The 'depths of despair' I have heard it called, well yes, you are at the depths of despair and then wandering down the ward, wanting death to overtake your steps and to take you before you reach the nurses station (an isolated oasis of dim light at the end of the ward by the doors, manned by the night nurses, usually three, and placed at a strategic position to observe most of the ward exits and entrances and to keep patients from escaping through the main doors), and, when this did not happen, and you reached the pool of light they sat in, one of them saying something like 'You all right Alyn, want a cuppa or a talk?' and then sitting quietly whilst hell in words and feelings spilled from you, listening patiently and more importantly with understanding to your personal hell, and when you had exhausted yourself of that night's burden and could say no more from sheer pain, them helping you back to bed with perhaps the crutch of a sleeping pill, tucking you in and you then falling into a chemically-induced oblivion of escape from it all, awakening halfway through the next day to one of the day staff saying, 'Heard you had a bad night, Alyn, so we left you to lie in, how do you feel?' God bless them, God bless them.

I have stayed many times in a mental health unit amongst the broken and insane, I have seen and felt the torment of these people, have been one of them, lived with them, and most of all learned from them. I am not alone, and that means a lot to me. Life's events broke me – they have broken others too, before me, and after me.

Waking on the ward, not knowing what day it is, sitting in the breakfast room whilst it is served, not being allowed to go off the ward to the main dining area for fear of them not being able to stop you committing suicide, ending the life they fought so hard to keep going, and knowing you are being watched every minute, with love and care until you stop feeling those feelings and later, watching from your crutch of temporary levelness, others in the same place you were, taking their turn to be watched. Ordinary people, mostly just like you, each with their own particular hang-up, phobia or nightmare. That makes you grow in a way you never thought possible before. Thank you, staff of those wards.

Thank you also for keeping me alive.

Confronting those ghosts and ghoulies then? Harder, much, much harder, starting to 'feel' again, and when I say 'feel' I mean being able to separate truth from nightmare; reality from retreat into madness was at first an impossibility to me. I wasn't starting to feel again, I was starting to feel for the first time, I had never allowed myself feelings; I had 'hidden' inside myself. I had escaped my life of pain by switching off, so here I was, a 40-year-old man with no previous experience of being a person. I had always been what others wanted me to be, the father, the husband, the provider, the lover, the sex object. Facing the past now. Wow, I am still not there but back then. I have trouble even now in comprehending what it was like, insurmountable, impossible, unobtainable, and that's where the shrinks came in. I hate them all, and yet without them I would still be insane.

Imagine a mirror, one in which when you looked every single line, crack and cranny, pore, crease and spot, every tiny imperfection was shown there, you could stand a mile away or an inch and still you got the same view. You could put on as much foundation, or as much soap on your face or steam the mirror over totally, still you would see every imperfection every time you looked at yourself. That's what shrinks do.

They don't tell you anything, they don't force you into anything, you're not told to do anything; they just talk to you, and when you talk to them you're looking at the mirror. No hiding place, it's there in front of you, and that can be so painful. Slowly, slowly at your own pace, they start to unravel you. What starts out as spaghetti becomes a tangled ball of wool, then a spool of string, then a length of twine. When you're fully unwound they help you to roll up the twine into manageable balls and put it away somewhere it won't become tangled again.

I hate them because they give no mercy, hold no punches, they show you yourself, and if yourself is not very good that's not a very nice thing. I am about at the ball of string stage, but more of that later.

It took months of patient meetings to get me to open up a fraction. I have no doubt they saw it all from day one, but to me it took what seemed like an eternity to fit the contact lenses on my head that allowed me to even recognise what was wrong with me, because all I knew was I didn't know. I just could not figure anything out, everything was such a jumble, up was down, black was white and bad was good.

One thing I did do, I changed my name.

The name on this book is MY name, who I am, who I became from the non-person I was before. I have changed all the other previous names to protect those I have already hurt from further harm. I have become me. It took a year of intense therapy to get that far, each day tearing down another little bit of the past, the abuse, my parents, my twin – there was a lot of stuff there to wade through, there still is, but to create a firm footing to start from I felt I should start from scratch, not absolve myself from blame but to stand in a place I could at least feel a firm floor under myself.

I had always hated my old name (I still cannot say that name openly without great difficulty, I hated him, me, then), my family had gone, my parents were dead, I had no contact with my brothers or sister; it was the perfect opportunity to do so. Nanin had suffered all that stuff, I could not make him clean, he, I was drowning. To have any hope at all I needed an island, a safe place to stand. I climbed out of the sea of insanity that day and stood for the first time in the sunlight, still wet, still unable to move from my island, still surrounded by a sea of insanity (my past), but Nanin was safe. I was safe, I had something completely mine, untouched by anyone or anything else – I had my name, and in changing my name a new line of my life opened, and in doing so, yet another two things happened.

I went on holiday and I fell in love.

PARADISE

I had been going to therapy and seeing shrinks for about a year. In between there were stays in hospital, the divorce, failed suicide attempts and trying to come to terms with the massive upheaval my life had taken. In those dark days when there seemed to be perpetual night all around me I did not look forwards: I looked, when I could bear the pain, to the past. I knew I had to empty the room full of ghosts I had accumulated, as at this time, they lived with me daily, hourly, each and every second in fact. I was in hell, living waking hell. I was almost glad (almost) that my family was not there – I did not want ANYONE to see me like this, the mask had been ripped forcibly off my face, I was there for all to see, naked once again, but not just my body was vulnerable, my very thoughts seemed to be too.

I had been having some quite bad sessions in therapy, I was having flashbacks of Jeff, my father, I would be walking down a road and a smell or sight would take me right back instantaneously to a previous time and I would find myself sweating and cowering against the wall or hedge, unable to control myself. I remember once being in the middle of town, and someone walked by just talking to their friend, and the tone of the voice and the way they had interacted had me right back in that park that day, one person was fat, the other a similar build to Jeff, and I just broke down and started crying for no other reason. Great sobbing tears, it was so embarrassing. Some lady had to help me to a seat and a crowd started to gather, I didn't know what to do with myself, luckily a nurse from the hospital was passing and took me to her car and drove me to the Assessment Centre of the Mental Health Unit, where I stayed for several hours calming down. They said it was 'cathartic' and a sign I was dealing with things; I said it was most embarrassing and I hope it didn't happen again. All in all I was pretty worn out, when I did look in the mirror I looked haggard, old, I felt 90, weak and needed to rest for a year.

Jack and Jane had been my only visitors; they had kept in discreet touch, giving me space but letting me know they at least were there for me, if no one else was. They said I should think about a holiday. I had received a small settlement for the sale of my share of the house and I put the idea on the back burner for now until I could get round to it.

I kept my eye on the travel agent's windows though and shortly after saw a holiday in Rhodes, Greece, one week self-catering £135 all in. When I enquired it sounded nice, so I booked it for the following week. Jane organised my money being changed, Jack packed my suitcase, and they delivered me to the airport on the day with me literally dragging my feet. I was having cold feet about the whole thing, I was absolutely exhausted and really only wanted to go to sleep for a week. They guided me through the terminal, PUSHED me through the passport control barrier and told me to go and have a good time. There was no going back then: my case was loaded and I was past the point of no return.

I sat in the departure lounge in a semi-trance.

Somewhere, someone up there must have been looking over me.

I think a combination of everything had brought me to a point where everything was in liquid transition. I had no base to work from, I didn't know who I was, what I wanted, or where to go to get it. I vaguely remember my flight being called, getting on the plane, it taking off and then ... I was up there in the sky, above the clouds, almost like I was in heaven, above everything looking down, I could see (in my mind's eye) the whole thing. I felt the need to re-invent myself, to BECOME someone, so I did, it just popped into my head, simply and easily: I would start afresh, wipe the board, change my name.

CHANGE MY NAME. God that was it, I was who I was. That was my name, me, and that was all crap, pain and terror. I would give myself a name that I chose, not that was chosen for me, I would be ... TONY THORNTON.

78

I landed at Rhodes, and when the pilot announced our arrival the name of the airport he said it was 'Paradisi' in Greek, in English 'Paradise'. I had landed in Paradise.

It was close to 3 a.m. when I got to my hotel, closer to 4 a.m. when settled into my room. I had given my passport in as normal, and about an hour later with me sitting on my balcony, with a stunning view of the mountains and trees in front, feeling the warm foreign air on my face, the door was knocked on gently. I opened it to find the lady owner there, who said with apologies she was just checking if I was still awake as she had noticed on my passport that it was my birthday today, and as I was alone would I accept from the hotel this card, bottle of wine and salad as a tribute to it, mumbling something about 'all she could rustle up at this hour'. My birthday, my God, I had forgotten all about it. I gave her my thanks, returned to the balcony with my gifts, and in realising what day it was and knowing Jack and Jane had packed for me, opened my suitcase to find a card there from them too.

After Christmases with my boys, there is one other memory that will be with me forever, that morning, sat on the balcony in the warm, drinking a glass of retsina wine, nibbling on a Greek salad with a card from Jack and Jane and one from the hotel in front of me, watching the sun come up over the hills. You know at the end of the old cowboy films when the sun comes up over the hill and a new day is born and you just know that all will be rosy in the characters' future from then on, and that this is the start of something new and wonderful; well I felt like that. I had been in the clouds, been as close to heaven as it is possible to get whilst still living, and had landed, purely by chance, on my birthday, in paradise.

I defy anyone to tell me this was not fate's hand; the island I spoke of was almost a real island, Rhodes. I was reborn, I was TONY THORNTON, I had a base to work from, I was a PERSON.

The rest of the holiday was great. I relaxed, unwound and for seven short days put the world somewhere else. I took time for the first time in my life, for ME. The mask was in England, I was here, the old me? Well, I would sort that out later, but for now I could just be me. I loved it

I almost did a 'Shirley Valentine' whilst there: a couple who part ran the hotel were looking for someone to run their video rental and scuba shop, the job came with a small hut/room on the beach and the facilities of the hotel, plus a small wage, and they offered it to me, to ME, not the mask. I was very, very tempted and sat, like Shirley, on the beach that last day, contemplating whether to take up the offer, but I needed to sort out my life. I felt for the first time a need to get well and to sort myself out. I got on the plane that day full of hope.

I returned to England refreshed and revived; it all hit me again upon my return, but this time I had a standpoint, I changed my name legally through a solicitor two days after returning and for the first time EVER, I was looking forward.

I started going out, I was still under intense therapy, but sitting in the flat night after night wasn't helping, so I slowly started off my social life again, not tarting it, but I found a club for single, separated and divorced (which I was by then) and started going weekly. As I have said, I had learned to present a good personality and did so again, that was part of me I wanted to keep. I therefore got on well at the club: within two weeks I was on the committee table and closely involved in things.

A few weeks after joining, I was sitting at our table when a lady sat down next to me at the behest of another committee member, as she was new and was trying to avoid the attention of a man who seemed to have taken a shine to her, but whom she was not interested in, so, as was usual, would sit with us for a few weeks to let things calm down. I paid no attention at first, didn't even look in her direction as I was in conversation with someone else at the time. I just knew from the corner of my eye she was there, what was going on and to 'shield' her slightly from this man. A couple of minutes later, my conversation having just ended, I felt her say 'Oh God, here he comes' and turn slightly towards me. We touched, I turned to her, she to me, I looked into her eyes for the first time, she into mine and I fell in love. It was like being hit by electricity.

Mills and Boon, huh. Love story, nahhh. I didn't believe any of it, things like that just do not happen, but here I was looking at this woman for the first time in my life, and I just knew. I just knew.

I watched *Sleepless in Seattle* some time afterwards; I was that

80

man, it happened to me. Unbelievably the impossible happened, I fell headlong in love, it felt like she was pulling the very heart out of me, like we were joined from the soul, ha, ha. I know how stupid this all sounds, ha, ha. But it was true. Perhaps because I had not HAD any proper feelings before, or maybe it was because I was no longer the mask, but me (well, I was a long way along the road to becoming me anyway), I allowed myself to fall in love. I don't know, I only know I did, and it was wonderful.

I had met and fell in love with Aly (Alyshia); she was lovely, blonde hair, blue eyes that sparkled when she looked at you. I melted every time I looked at her; I had overwhelming urges to take her in my arms and hold her, to tell her how much I loved her and cared for her. We 'fitted' each other in a way I didn't know was possible: touching fingers sent warm pulses through my body. I know, I know it all sounds sickening, doesn't it? Like a lovesick schoolboy's dream, well it was.

It was like nothing I had ever felt before; quote from the movie, 'I was just holding the door for her and we touched, and I knew, I just knew.' Well I knew, I just knew. She was the one.

Making love, I will only say a little about, something that special is not to be shared. I will only say, it was clean, wholesome and very, very fulfilling. Special is like describing the QE2 as a boat. This was VERY special. For once, my past was somewhere else, I felt clean, new and I loved her very, very much (I still do).

We lasted four years, and that was the most fulfilling four years of my life. I had found respect, I had found love, I had found someone who not only was clean and straight themselves but that treated me as clean and straight too. I have nothing but praise for this lady, for she is indeed a lady, refined but down to earth, soft but hard as nails when pushed, a divorced mother of three who did not crumble from life's knocks but stood up and fought her way through things with a poise and elegance I loved, still love this lady very, very, very much.

I could quote records, songs and poems galore that say what I felt. I felt the hero, the champion, she made me feel clean and respectable, she taught me without saying a word how to be me without compromising me, if you know what I mean. I did not have to 'be' anything, just myself, and that, in the end, was the downfall of our relationship.

She was clean, respectable and whole, and I was, well, I was what I was. A semi-reformed mental case with a past that shamed Lady Chatterley and her lovers.

I had become something else, but my past clung to me like a millstone.

She made me feel so good, though I used to have massive guilt attacks when we kissed, if only she knew what those lips had been made to do, when we made love and there, there dear reader is a huge event change, we made love, not sex, love. It was the most wonderful experience I had ever felt sexually, her too, she said. So clean, so wholesome but completely, completely satisfying for us both, but I had done things and had things done to me so bad that how could I then be clean with her, it felt like I contaminated her with my dirt.

She did not know this. I hid it well, but inside I felt it. I longed to tell her what had happened, did a little in fact, but saw, felt the change in her when mentioned. I wanted absolution, I wanted to be straight with her as she was with me, and it ate away at me like a cancer. We rowed often, broke up for weeks, months on end. I tried on one hand to be the person I wanted to be – clean, respectable, whole and mostly always with her. Oh, how I loved her, every time I looked at her, each time she passed into my thoughts I felt a swelling, a physical pulling of my heart for her. When in her arms, not even making love, just hugging, touching, being with each other, it was a touch of heaven. We used to sometimes just glance in passing at each other and each knew, felt that feeling. She opened to me like a flower starved of sunlight; I opened to her like day following night, and all in a glance. It was wonderful.

On the other hand, I was in and out of mental health units, going through untold agony of therapy and dealing with my worst nightmares coming true, my past being real and not just a bad dream, and trying to balance the two together at once. I just could not do it; I wanted help and understanding from Aly, but could not bear to tell her of my problems. I wanted to keep us 'clean' and whole.

She, on the other hand, sensed there was more to things but

only knew clean and whole, and I knew, as I said earlier, when you haven't had stuff like that in your life before, it becomes unfathomable to understand. I knew, I understood, but the daily frustration of living two lives became unbearable. Our relationship ended.

I learned loads from her; I owe her a debt of gratitude I will never be able to repay. But Aly, if you ever read this and know all the facts could you ever come to me, hold me in your arms, kiss me, take me to bed as your partner in love and spend the rest of your life with me, knowing, knowing the stuff that has happened to me? Knowing what I was – all that stuff, it happened to ME, to MY body, to MY mind, how could I ever be clean for you? When we were together I kept that as much apart from us as I could, I went to therapy every Monday as I still do and let out another bit of my past, and would come home to you after and put on the mask again, whilst all the time fighting to take the damn thing off for good and throw it away. You were clean, I felt dirty, I had found something so intensely wantable in you, I wanted to keep it forever, respectability and to do that, I had to keep part of me aside from us, again, whilst daily trying to put my past in its place. I was to you 'a nice man'; I was to myself the product of my past. I found with you an escape into cleanness; you had, have, the power to cure me, simply by loving me no matter what. By having faith in me and loving me 'even though' if you understand. I, on the other hand, have no right to ask something of you I know would be so difficult.

I have been touched by abuse, pain, insanity, I could not possibly ask anyone untouched by these things to voluntarily make contact with them even at second-hand for my benefit, so I hid it from you. I had tried to show Lisa and had hurt her, the next option was to keep it to myself, and that broke us.

I still love you Aly, very, very much. I have given you your freedom, terminated the relationship, I wish you happiness and health. You will perhaps meet someone else, go past me, move on. Bless you, I hope you do, but I don't think anyone will EVER love you like I do. Please forgive me and understand.

I hope you, the reader, will indulge me for a while here as I am full of unanswered questions. I presume most of you will be (I hope) unaffected in your life from what I lived with, and although I know there will be a few of you (hopefully more than a few of you will buy this book, ha, ha) who unfortunately will know all too well of what I write, and to those my heart goes out, I wonder then, if you have never had this in your life, how would you deal with contact with it? If someone close to you (partnership-wise) said after reading this 'Yes, that happened to me too', how would you cope? Take them in your arms, love them, be revolted by it, go away from them in sheer disgust, be unable to deal with it? How would you live with knowing all that had happened to the closest person to you? I would dearly love to know, as it would influence how I approached telling someone in the future.

And to you that have had this in your lives, how would you tell your partner, would you dare rock the boat or keep quiet? Hold the agony to yourselves to spare them, hope that they will save you how, how would you do it?

I give you an example. I have been apart from Aly for almost a year now, I feel a lot better, am still going to weekly therapy and am, albeit slowly, getting better. I have kept myself to myself, have almost hibernated, as because I am trying to deal with all this 'stuff' inside me, I feel I cannot give anything to anyone else until I am, what's the word, 'cured'? 'better'? 'okay with myself'? Anyway, I have just been on my own. I have a nice flat with a garden and have made it an oasis of safety in which to base my future security on. I have not been able to work because I cannot in all honesty at the moment say I will be able to give one whole complete week of 'normality' to an employer. I 'suffer' lots, I am in great pain from dealing with my past for the majority of the time. If you saw me in the street you would say 'You're looking good', but in reality you would be looking at the temporary mask I put on to be able to deal with essentials like shopping (otherwise I would literally starve) or paying bills etc. That is not the me who is indoors, the REAL me, the one struggling to come to terms with everything, so I live, I go on daily fighting to get well, to get 'level' and to survive all of this.

Through a neighbour's bereavement I recently met a woman, she is lovely and I have half-formed a friendship with her. I can offer almost nothing to it apart from friendship, but she seems happy with that. I know it could go further if I wanted, but right now I am not ready: for one thing I am still deeply in love with Aly, for another I have not come to terms with my past and still feel dirty and worthless. It brought up a question in me though, as I have said, how do you deal with this in relationships? At some-time (who knows when) in the future, I will feel ready to take up life again (I bloody hope so, anyway) and may meet someone. The old question comes up I heard so long ago from a fellow patient, 'How do you make a prostitute into a virgin?' How do I, having experienced all I have, kiss someone without the mask on with lips that have been forced to do 'that' and put what is the most private part of my body within someone else, in love's way, and whilst not living a lie, when it has had 'that' done to it? When I am on my own, as I am now, I am reasonably okay, I leave the 'mask' off and just use it for outside to hide my pain from others. So with it off and me exposed, how do I approach someone I may feel for and be in a relationship with them? Do I tell them? Do I keep it from them? How do I mix my body with them and still keep my sanity? Who will love me knowing what has happened to me?

When I look into myself, yes, I can do that now, I see me and I know I am a good person deep down. I am full of love; I feel loving feelings, not sexual, but warmth for others. I try to be a good neighbour, a good person, I help if I can, I am 'there' for people, and on the whole I am happy that I am growing into the person I always knew I wanted to be. I don't smoke, rarely drink (although I enjoy a glass of red wine greatly), I rarely swear (hammer on the thumb times perhaps) I keep my home clean and tidy, am 'domesticated', can go out and 'party' with the best of them (with the help of the mask) and am quite popular and liked by others.

I ask myself if I took off the mask for good and showed others the pain I feel, as I tried with Lisa, what would happen? Who would love the real me if I showed them me? Who would love me then?

THE BIG PICTURE

So many things, so much hurt.

The doctors have said, 'Look at the big picture', so I do. I think it falls into two categories, the people in my life and how those people have influenced my life.

I once said, and mean, that 'out there' in life, I can deal with things. Joe Blow citizen and their dog do not worry me, I put the mask on so they will not see my vulnerability, and I owe them nothing, and they owe me nothing. I interact with them on a one-to-one equal basis. If in passing I can do a good turn and it will cost me little or nothing, then so be it. Inside myself, I KNOW I am a good person; I bear no ill will or malice to anyone out there.

There are, however, 15 to 20 people in my inner circle of life who I cannot deal with, those closest to me, who are able to deal me more harm than the rest of the world put together.

I am told my need for love that was denied at an early age has weakened my strength and courage to deal with love and affection now. I would not argue with that. I 'fall over' at regular intervals with those close to me, barely cope with those that ARE close to me, and don't come close to coping with the closest thing to me, relationships.

I have had two wonderful women in my life, and whilst I did not love Lisa the way I love Aly, I managed to lose both of them. They say 'good guys come last', they also say the world loves a winner, smile and the world smiles with you, cry and you cry alone. I have found both to be true.

I am a male. I suppose I am typical of the species. I would categorise myself as 'new age liberal', whatever that means! I care about people, I believe in equality and try to treat the opposite sex as courteously as possible. I open doors, hold coats whilst being put on and generally buy the drinks, whilst going halves if that's what is wanted. I halve the housework, cook and clean, and am just as likely to run a hot bath for my partner if I know she has had a bad day, as I am to listen to the offload of moans from them if they need it. I prepare romantic meals, small surprises like a note secretly tucked in her lunch pack saying 'I love you', and try to make her feel 'special' every now and then with a bunch of flowers or box of chocs when least expected. I am not perfect, far from it, to pay for the 'gentleman' in me, I have not a few hang-ups, I am insecure (very), I am probably a little over-demanding for affection at times (not sex, just cuddles), and know I can be a moody git at times. To me, from a male point of view, I will trade my good and bad for a woman's good and bad, PMT and all, but have found that even my best attempts to please even at times of extreme stress in my partner's world, are not credit enough in the bank of relationship to pay for me being in need of help when the times comes. I get 'dumped' at regular intervals and wonder if I am doing it right after all.

I believe in the words of the wedding vows, 'for better or worse, richer or poorer, sickness and in health', if I love that person, I will stick by them through thick or thin, backing them every inch of the way and taking, if necessary, the bullets aimed at them. In my whole life though, sad to say, I have never enjoyed the same back, and whilst that is no indictment on the female sex as a whole, the ones I have been with certainly have not been there for me.

My shrink says I 'give' too much too soon and then expect the same back. She says I should learn to give in proportion to what I get, making an even trade, that my need for love drives me to seek it by 'prepayment' methods, I give therefore you must give, and that does not work. I guess I am still pretty screwed up in that area; my younger years, when I should have been going through trial and error phases with girls, were otherwise taken up. My guideline for affection was give 100 per cent and maybe I would get 10 per cent back, learn to quickly ascertain and fulfil others' desires, and they might thank you with pseudo-love.

I got in contact with an organisation in Sheffield called

Survivors; they sent me a booklet on how to survive abuse. It was fascinating, every page I went 'Yeah, I know THAT feeling'; it seems there are hundreds of us out there, half of me is glad I am not alone, half is sad there are so many of us.

How the hell do I get back to what is supposedly 'normal'? I want to be married to a woman that loves me and to love her; more importantly I want respect between us, to know we will not give hurt to each other and will live the rest of our lives out in togetherness, no matter what. Is that too romantic a request to make because at every turn I seem to get further from that?

This last Christmas, one of my sons, who I know is still struggling to deal with the hurt of his life being thrown upside down by his mum and me divorcing, 'chucked a wobbly', and, I presume, to get back at me for the hurt I caused in his life, fought with me and put me into hospital for Christmas Day and Boxing Day: he beat me up pretty badly with a baseball bat. The staff in hospital found it hard to understand why; I didn't. I wish I had done the same to my father; maybe him getting it out of his system that way will save him from years of therapy later, who knows. I only know I love him still. He contacted me a week later whilst just having been beaten up himself after getting drunk, New Year's Eve in fact, and I went and rescued him; he never spoke of the week before, but in leaving my car came back to the window, leaned in and said 'Love you dad, thanks.' I guess he is fighting his own devils right now, and I hope he knows whilst I need a 'sorry' from him before we return to normal relations, I do understand and I will ALWAYS be there for him.

Trouble is, there is never anybody there for me, doctors yes, nurses, the odd friend even (J&J), but within that close circle of me I can rely on no one. I remember in hospital one time I had to walk to the main block in my hospital jamas to buy a shirt and jeans from the shop there as my sons would not visit me and bring in clothes from my flat, it seemed to be too much trouble for them. I am, however, expected to be there for them every time. I had a long talk about primary/secondary relationships whilst in therapy, and know I have a lot to learn there too.

It took a long time to learn I need to put into place boundaries for my family. I have a responsibility as a parent, maybe too late, to put into place a 'safety net' on which one side is acceptable and the other unacceptable, and in which they know beyond all doubt they can rely on. I gave my sons everything, I spoiled them rotten to make up for my childhood, then later I ruled them with an iron rod, how the hell then can they know what is right and what is wrong? I gave no firm boundaries but moved them to suit my current circumstance. I will put that right now. I will give an unbending guideline for them to know: whether they follow it is up to them, they are all grown up now and make their own decisions. I have said to each of them over time, do what you feel is best but take the consequence, good or bad, for your actions. I hope I have taken mine and in setting these boundaries am doing the right thing albeit a little late. I am crap at dealing with these things, but will do all in my power to learn.

My sons; well, the eldest is in Australia, and whilst he is full of insecurity he knows I am there for him and I love him, we have a good long-distance relationship. The next is the one who fought with me, my heart goes out to him, he deals with life by being 'Mr Tough Guy'. I hope someday he forgives me. The next I have a really close relationship with; of all my sons (and I love them equally) he is closest purely because we share so much in common. The youngest, he is not yet 'in there', having only recently flown the nest from his mum's, we are still I feel a little distant, he is still weighing up the person I am, from the person I was; he said once, 'Dad, I hated the old you but I would do anything for the new you' – praise indeed!

So there is hope for us all yet. The biggest feelings I have inside are of being a dad and a homemaker, I would love to be a partner, no, a 'husband' to someone eventually, but we will see. I hurt daily at the torment I feel for my family – if I had one wish it would be to put right the damage I have done to them. I can rationalise it by saying it is because of my past experiences, but that does not make things right, and I want so much for the line of hurt to stop at this level and not carry on to the next generation.

I hurt daily at the things that have been done to me. I 'comfort eat' and am currently at 15 stone, two stone overweight; it does not make up for love, but fills my stomach instead of my heart, so will do for now. I plod through the debris of my life and try to make some sense of it, I learn daily to respect myself, to try and become 'clean', I am not there yet.

Twelve years ago, my parents and Jeff died, nine years ago I got divorced, 47 years ago I was physically born, eight years ago I was mentally 'born'.

I figure I have around (with luck) another 20 odd years of life left. I wonder what they will bring.

I was born Alyn Joseph Wilson (made-up name), 'Nanin' (true nickname); I am now Tony Thornton.

The interaction between past relationships, my father, mother, grandfather, grandmother, uncle was a mess. It is said my grand-dad is my brother's father, it is said my father slept with my grand-mother in revenge. It is said my father beat my mother. It is said he killed my unborn twin (and possibly other unborn babies) from those beatings. It is said he was bisexual, sleeping with his sergeant to avoid heavy duties (the front line supposedly), but that he only did it to stay alive. It is said my mother was 'easy' because of my grandfather's abuse. It is said my Uncle Jeff was like he was for the same reason. It is said there is a streak of 'that' running right through our family and that unless the bloodline finishes, will continue to run.

I know some of this to be absolutely true by first-hand experi-ence. I know that 'that' has run through me to some extent. I have NEVER sexually abused my sons, but did my wife, physically and sexually, as I did Sarah that time. I do know there is the ability to stop a line of this type dead. I have done it. A leopard never changes its spots, it is said. I have. Alyn Joseph Wilson is no more; in truth he never really existed. Nanin, the little boy in the mask, took all the hurt. I am he, all grown up now, and I have taken off the mask, I cannot throw it away yet, but that day will come. I could put down all the excuses for the others, perhaps the abuse goes back another generation, perhaps they too were unable to deal with life events, perhaps, perhaps, perhaps.

The fact is it happened. I cannot change the past for me person-ally. The little boy called Nanin that was me went through what he did, it happened. I was raped orally, many many times, I was abused sexually many many times, I was abused mentally for almost all of my life, I was unwanted and unloved by my father certainly, by my mother – I think she just gave up. I spent many hours stuck up the side of a fridge watching the world go by and not being part of it. I was battered to 'nothing' over a long period of time. I held the guilt of my dead twin, my mother's miscarriages and her stays in hospital along with not feeling like a man, being immensely inadequate and a failure at being a husband, father and provider of normality for my family.

I failed my girlfriend, I failed myself, I failed to see the signs and put things right in time. I could beat myself up for ever and ever, the facts are it happened.

I have lived every minute of my pain out; I am confronting every single skeleton in my cupboard. I have wrenched, pulled and dug out with a rusty nail every single ordeal I have been through, and it has nearly killed me in the process.

I am still not there; I still go weekly to therapy. On a scale of one to ten I am about seven. I have been celibate for almost a year since breaking with Aly. I have at least some respect finally for myself, my body belongs to ME, and I will share it with only those I choose. I am growing to accept myself and more importantly, like myself.

Mum and dad are dead, Jeff is dead, my older brother, Lawrence, has moved away and got married and had children. I see almost nothing of him; he has his own life now away from his own devil memories. Mickey is also married with children, I see nothing of him: we have absolutely nothing in common, he was the golden boy, the 'first born' and along with that, came a respectability I could never obtain. Dee is also similarly fixed, Dad left all his money to her, as a final act of family wrenching apart, that tear will never heal. I bear her no harm and wish her well, she could no more help being born a girl than I could help being born a boy, but she was one of four children, and dad cutting three of us off and giving to one, was to me the final act of hurt he could do. I do not care about the money; it is being not in there and again rejected that hurt the most. I found my twin, yes, I dug and dug after being told that she had been 'thrown in someone else's grave' by dad, found she had not at all, she has a grave of her own in a mass baby grave, I had the exact spot marked by the staff there – 'thank you', and visit her often. When I sit on the grass by her I feel not alone anymore, does that sound silly? It's as if she is saying to me 'I am down here, you are up there breathing air and living, go out and live for both of us.' So I try.

I grow stronger each day, both mentally and spiritually. I am not a 'God' person, religion has not bitten me, but I believe in something, too much has happened in my life for me to say it is not so, there is something out there and I feel watched over sometimes. I half hope it is you, dad, and that in heaven or wherever it is, you finally love me now, oh well, you can only hope, eh.

I have my sons and I love them dearly, although I am now a person and not the same thing they had as a father, that bond of paternity is just as strong in me, stronger even, and I have to daily stop myself from 'making up' for the past hurt by shepherding their lives – they are all grown up now and able to take care of themselves thankfully. I don't think they know the full story; they will if they ever read this. I hope, like Lisa and Aly, they do understand and perhaps forgive me a little. The little boy Nanin is almost grown up now, I still see a path ahead to normality and will follow it to its end.

I could finish by giving you a million and one other examples of past hurts, but what would that achieve? I thank you for sharing these with me; to give you more would burden you unnecessarily.

Nanin was hurt badly; I am nearly better.

I hope the hurt I gave others along the way heals quickly too. The future, yes, I look to the future now, for my sons I will try and be a good dad and 'be there' for them whenever they want. For myself, the thing I would still like most is to be loved. I know my lads love me, but I mean love for ME by someone special, who, though would want me, what woman would kiss and hug me after what has happened?. As I said, in therapy once someone said, 'How do you make a prostitute into a virgin again?' I guess you can't. I am what I am. I live in hope of someone accepting me for that and wanting to spend their old age with me anyway. Something else though, that feeling, the one I had with Aly, that is something special, will I ever feel that again? Who knows?

Ruined lives, there have been a few, but ruined up till now. A ruined thing can be rebuilt as long as the foundations are okay and if, like me, you have no foundations, then build some so you don't fall down again.

To my lovely wife I say sorry, you were part of my life for a long time. I hurt you badly and ask not for forgiveness but understanding. I hope now you do understand. I wish you well despite all that has happened, Lisa, I still care for you and will be here if you ever need me.

To my children, I fell off the line boys, and there was no one there to catch me, no excuse for what happened. I was, am your dad, and I should have been there for you always. I hope you know whatever has happened, and whatever happens in the future I love you all very much.

To Aly, I love you honey, I always have. If you can find it in your heart to understand, then please try. No man (or woman) is an island, we all need something, sometime, I just needed more than you could give, eh. You gave me hope, you showed me respect, and I love you even more for that.

To my parents, I forgive you.

To Jeff, I hope from the flames of hell's worst fire, you look up and see me laughing at you, you bastard, may you suffer an eternity of agony.

Guess I still have a way to go, eh!

EPILOGUE

After writing this book, I had a few copies made into manuscript form and, after discussing it with the group, sent one or two off to publishers for consideration for publishing. The fact you are reading this now means I was successful and am now an author.

I sent a copy to Aly also, as I did to my sons. The response I got from them surprised me, and it was a very positive one.

About a week after sending Aly a copy, I had a ring at my door; it was her. I let her in rather shakily, as we had been apart for some time then. As we stood in the lounge, looking at each other warily, she took me in her arms, kissed me, and told me the words I had always wanted to hear, that she loved me. To me, my dream had come true. We talked, and all of a sudden, it all came tumbling out, I started sobbing uncontrollably, and for every word I said, she gave back acceptance, as all the past hurt and pain came out, she let me know that I was loved. We went to bed, and made love, clean, lovely untouched from the past love, and lay after in a peace I have rarely known. We made plans for the future together, and for the first time in my life I felt hope.

We went away on holiday shortly after, and had a wonderful week in the sun together, but when we returned home from it, I felt a change in her, she no longer talked of the future, and seemed to withdraw somewhat from us as a couple. I found more and more that my life was drawn to her side of things, whilst less and less was invested in mine. It came to a head about a month later. I had gone out and booked further holidays for the future, and had spent almost all my time at her place to try to show the commitment I felt was not being returned, but I knew in my heart that the inevitable was again happening. I got pretty low, and, when you feel like that, your resistance to illness reduces, I caught a flu-like virus that was prevalent in the city at that time, and spent a week at my flat feeling pretty ill. Again, I was on my own for it, no contact from Aly, no 'are you alright?' 'Haven't seen you for a week' – nothing.

I found a strength in me that week. My spirit plummeted at first, and I thought, 'oh no, it's happening again' rejection, then it was as if an answer popped into my head from nowhere: NO, BE STRONG. I knew that she had felt sorry for me, had knocked on my door in sympathy, not love, had tried again in our relationship out of compassion, not because she wanted me, but because she wanted to make me feel better, and that was ok, I understood that. When we had been together for a bit, had a nice holiday etc, it had worn off for her, and I felt she didn't know how to put me down again after picking me up. There was a difference now though. I was stronger, I didn't need picking up. I had learnt to stand on my own two feet finally.

Well, Aly and I are no longer together, it has ended. I still love her, very very much, but a relationship has to be two way, and my whole life had been based on one way relationships. I gave, they took. No more, no more. I am back to where I was at the end of the last chapter, but with one important difference, a big piece of the jigsaw has finally slotted into place in me; I know where the plimsoll line is now – you know, the line on a boat that makes the difference between floating and sinking. I know where to draw that line in relationships now, and should I be lucky enough to find someone in the future who will not only accept me for who and what I am but love me with a passion to match my own, then that knowledge will figure heavily in keeping us afloat I feel.

One more thing, looking back on this book. I have made excuses for all the stuff and all the people in it, no one has been to blame except me, I have to say this. If I look inside myself, I see only love, kindness and caring, there is no bitterness or hatred, no guilt or regrets, I am at one with myself finally, and have put into place the means to be at peace with myself too.

I have arranged a trip to Australia, to see my son. Whilst there, the little boy Nanin in me is going to die. I am going to let him go peacefully, his time of pain is at an end, the blackness that has filled my life has all been dug out. The last bit, his spirit, I am going to lay to rest on some beach on the barrier reef coast, where, in my mind, I can think of him spending eternity amongst the palm trees and coral reefs.

I made a small clay model of me being born whilst in early therapy; it brought out a tremendous surge of release when I made it. My therapist at the time said to keep it until I was sure the damage there was mended, then to bury it somewhere nice and let it go forever. He, it, me – that part of me – will be buried for eternity there, in the closest place I can find to heaven for it whilst living. It will be time for me then, no more past, just the future. I am crying again in writing this, for it is like knowing a piece of me is going to die, as indeed it is. I grieve for that piece, all that pain, all that blackness, and finally knowing peace and contentment for it, fills me with sadness, but also hope.

I have become a person finally, not only that, I have become the kind of person I always wanted to be, a good person. I use three words in my everyday working to give a guideline to my life: Strength, Courage, and Harmony. With those at your side, you can't go far wrong.

The saddest thing I write is, that apart from shrinks and doctors, I have had to do it all on my own, and for all the love I have given out in my life, no one has loved me enough to be there with me through it.

I don't know if there is a God? I only know that I thank whatever is there that I still feel love, am still full of love, and hope that someday, I may share that love with someone who will love me too.

So, I end this true story.

I hope you look back over this book and see the pain that has filled my life, and also the strength and courage it has taken, not only to face that pain, but to conquer it too.

I write it to let anyone out there who also faces pain, in what ever form, know that they are not alone, that if I can do it, so can you.

Whatever has happened to your body, and affected your mind,

96

your spirit is still yours, and can never be touched. Inside you, if you care to look, is a white shining love that will fill your very existence if you let it.

At my very first session with a shrink I was asked, 'What do you see inside yourself?' I answered a hard black dead hole.

Now I see a lightbulb burning so bright it outshines the sun.